SPOTLIGHT ON THE COLLEGE STUDENT

SPOTLIGHT on the

COLLEGE STUDENT

A DISCUSSION by the Problems and Policies Committee
of the American Council on Education

LED BY   DAVID RIESMAN   ·   PHILIP E. JACOB
NEVITT SANFORD

EDITED BY   MARGARET L. HABEIN

75528

AMERICAN COUNCIL ON EDUCATION   ·   Washington, D.C.

PRINTED IN THE UNITED STATES OF AMERICA

Foreword

THE PROBLEMS AND POLICIES COMMITTEE of the American Council on Education is a group of distinguished leaders in various sectors of American education elected by the membership to consider problems and issues of general concern to educational institutions and organizations. The meeting reported here was arranged at the suggestion of Dr. James R. Killian, Jr., then president of the Massachusetts Institute of Technology, and chairman of the committee.

Typically, the committee invites to its meetings one or more informed persons who speak on the issues and then participate in the discussion with members of the committee and with the Council officers and committee chairmen who are regularly invited. In the present instance, members of the committee believed that the opening presentations of Drs. Riesman, Jacob, and Sanford, together with an edited report of the discussion that followed, would present numerous ideas both provocative and useful to educators in American high schools, colleges, and universities. It is to be noted that no committee judgments were sought nor recorded in respect to the issues under debate. The report is published in the hope that it may help stimulate the kind of reflection at the campus level that the several contributions stimulated at the meeting itself.

Special thanks are due the three discussion leaders, who contributed valuable information and perceptive judgments; Dean Margaret L. Habein, whose skillful editing has made the discussion more coherent in print than it was in fact; and the Hazen Foundation, which provided the necessary funds for publication.

ARTHUR S. ADAMS, *President*
American Council on Education

February 11, 1959

Contents

Participants in the Discussion

THE ORAL DISCUSSION on which this book is based took place in June 1957. This fact has no significant effect on the currency of the ideas expressed because the speakers have had the opportunity, in recent months, to revise their remarks and, when necessary, bring them up to date. The names appear in the order in which speakers enter the discussion; some of the participants have had changes in position which are indicated below.

James R. Killian, Jr. Then President, Massachusetts Institute of Technology, and Chairman, Problems and Policies Committee; now Special Assistant to the President of the United States for Science and Technology.

David Riesman. Then Professor of Social Sciences, University of Chicago, and guest of the committee; now Henry Ford II Professor of Social Sciences at Harvard University.

Clark Kerr. Then Chancellor, University of California, Berkeley; now President, University of California. A member of the committee.

Raymond F. Howes. Staff Associate and Administrative Assistant, American Council on Education.

Sarah Goddard. Student Body President, Vassar College, Class of 1957, and a guest of the committee.

Philip E. Jacob. Professor of Political Science, University of Pennsylvania, and a guest of the committee.

Harry D. Gideonse. President, Brooklyn College, and a member of the committee.

Harald C. Bakken. Then President, United States National Student Association, and a guest of the committee.

Joseph C. McLain. Principal, Mamaroneck Senior High School, and a member of the committee.

W. Max Wise. Professor of Education, Teachers College, Columbia University, a member of the Council's Commission on the College Student, and a guest of the committee.

Douglas M. Knight.   President, Lawrence College, and a member of the committee.

Nevitt Sanford.   Professor of Psychology, University of California, Berkeley; Coordinator, Mary C. Mellon Foundation Program, Vassar College, and a guest of the committee.

Nathan M. Pusey.   President, Harvard University, and a member of the committee.

Elmer Ellis.   President, University of Missouri, Chairman of the Council's Commission on Instruction and Evaluation, and a guest of the committee.

Frank C. Abbott.   Then Staff Associate, American Council on Education; now Assistant Dean of the University, Bucknell University.

Margaret L. Habein.   Dean, Fairmount College of Liberal Arts and Sciences, University of Wichita.

Background for the Discussion

Changing Values in College, the report prepared by Dr. Philip E. Jacob of the University of Pennsylvania, was a principal element in the background for the present discussion. All participants had read the report immediately prior to the meeting, and the main presentations and discussion reflect familiarity with its contents. A brief summary, authorized by Dr. Jacob and drawn from his article in the NEA *Journal, January 1958, is presented below. The full report is published by Harper and Brothers.*

Does Higher Education Influence Student Values?

PHILIP E. JACOB

A STUDY of what happens to the values of American students of today shows that their college experience barely touches their standards of behavior, quality of judgment, sense of social responsibility, perspicacity of understanding, and guiding beliefs.

This means that if institutions of higher learning are expected to fulfill the historic humanistic mission of what we have called liberal education, they will have to learn how to do it. They are *not* doing it now with most of their students.

This conclusion stems from an analysis of three main types of data, which social scientists obtained from over 100 institutions: studies of student attitudes conducted during the last 15 years, recent evaluations of the outcomes of general education and other courses and of various methods of teaching, and a number of comprehensive self-studies by particular institutions.

Fortunately, not all evidence is negative. There are some institutions in which students' values seem to develop, some teach-

3

ers whose influence penetrates and stays, and some educational techniques which help open the sensibilities as well as the intellectual perceptions of some students. But the prevailing situation concerning the influence of college on contemporary student values is as follows:

1. The values of American college students are remarkably homogeneous, considering the variety of their backgrounds and their relatively unrestricted opportunities for freedom of thought and personal development.

2. The main effect of higher education upon student values is to bring about general acceptance of a body of standards and attitudes characteristic of college-bred men and women in America.

3. For the most part, students' values do not vary greatly whether they have pursued a conventional liberal-arts program, an integrated general-education curriculum, or a professional-vocational option.

4. Quality of teaching has little effect upon the value-outcomes of students' general education.

5. The method of instruction seems to have only a minor influence on students' value judgments.

6. Similar as the patterns of student values appear on a mass view, the intellectual, cultural, or moral climate of some institutions stands out as having a peculiar potency.

7. Recent research has identified certain personality characteristics of students which filter their educational experiences.

The points presented here imply that no specific curricular pattern of liberal education, no pedigree of instructor, and no wizardry of instructional method should be patented for its impact on students' values. Indeed, the impact of American higher education as a whole upon the value patterns of college youth as a whole seems negligible.

The values of some students do change in college. But even with these, the impetus to change does not come primarily from the formal educational process. It comes from the distinctive climate of a few institutions, the individual and personal magnetism of a sensitive teacher with strong values, or the value-laden personal experiences which students occasionally undergo during college.

In short, college can contribute to the growth of a student's values only when it penetrates the core of his life and confronts him with fresh and often disturbing implications, which are different from those which he and his society have taken for granted. This can hardly occur as a by-product of a curricular assembly line. It requires a highly personal relationship between the college community and the individual student—a relationship that is warm and considerate, but at the same time mutually aggravating.

Introduction to the Subject

JAMES R. KILLIAN, JR.

THE TOPIC for discussion today is, broadly, the changing values of college students. What is happening, or has been happening, to American students? Have they been undergoing changes in attitudes and values which we as educators ought to understand and take into account as we plan our academic programs?

There have been many serious efforts to chart these changes and to describe them; my own personal reaction is that there have been a lot of easy generalizations made about student values that are almost becoming clichés in discussions today.

We hear on all sides that the college students are primarily interested in security and that they have lost their sense of risk-taking and of adventure. We hear this in industry, we hear it in academic circles, and we hear it in many other places. I sometimes wonder whether easy generalizations of this kind may not reflect more our own versions of what we think the students are thinking today rather than what they actually may be thinking or the attitudes they actually have.

I would also hope that we might consider whether this whole question of values is one for which we may develop a theory of indeterminacy, as we have in physics. There the mere act of observing attitudes and values may lead to misinterpretations because of the inevitable coloring and filtering by the observer who is trying to delineate what these values are or what changes may be taking place.

The whole discussion is going to be in part brought into focus by the exceedingly interesting research report that Dr. Jacob published recently as a result of the program he undertook, sponsored by the Hazen Foundation. His report has had a wide circulation in academic circles. Professor Jacob has attempted to bring together all the existing surveys and material he could find in an effort to draw some conclusions on whether, as I understand it, programs in social sciences in colleges have any effect upon the values of the students who take them. Do they cause these students to change their points of view? We are going to let him speak for himself later on.

There is another matter, about which discussion is widespread at the present time. In our academic programs at the undergraduate level, particularly, we are not in most of our institutions giving adequate attention to the subjects of personality and emotions and their impact on the educational progress of young people. Many people in the fields of psychiatry and psychology feel strongly that this is a relatively unexploited field and that we need to have a more scientific understanding of these things and their impact upon our educational programs.

But there is an adverse reaction, too, when one begins to talk about this subject. Some say that there is a grave hazard, not only in academic life, but in other kinds of institutional life as well, of developing bureaucracies because all these new methods of understanding which we think are important are requiring larger and larger organizations and more and more personnel to deal with them. Over and against this is the strong conviction on the part of many people that there are important things that we must do if we are really going to achieve an understanding of the ways in which we can most effectively make our educational programs work in behalf of the student and that this is going to require new approaches that we are not now utilizing.

As I see it, these are but a few of the issues that I hope we can look at in some detail. In order to get us started we will ask Dr. Riesman if he will lead off with some comments. I understand that some of his comments will be directed at Dr. Jacob's study. Then we hope that we may have some discussion.

Student Culture and Faculty Values

DAVID RIESMAN

IN HIS REPORT Dr. Jacob refers to a book, *Communism, Conformity and Civil Liberties* by Samuel Stouffer, which came out about a year ago and in which he polls the population at large on their attitudes toward academic freedom and like matters.[1]

The infiltration of tolerance

If one tries to put the Jacob report and the Stouffer report together, one finds a curious paradox. There isn't any doubt in the Stouffer report that the college population is slightly less bigoted than the general population, that college does have a loosening and liberating influence, which is most radically visible in the South. This is so, even though the Southern colleges in the Jacob report show up as the least emancipated in comparison with the Northern colleges; nevertheless, the Southerner who takes the giant step and goes through four years of college moves further away from his home environment (as represented by people who have finished high school only or have had but a short exposure to college) and closer to the values shared in general by the college-educated in this country than any other group in America who go to college, especially the group in the Far West where the general atmosphere of "tolerance" prevails widely among all strata. (I put "tolerance" in quotes, as I am sure Dr. Sanford would suggest on the basis of his own work.) There, also, the effect of college is not so drastic as in the South.

In trying to think about how one can reconcile this finding, which Dr. Jacob discusses, with the other material he discusses, showing the relative lack of impact of the college on its constituency, on the movement of minds in the college, it seemed to me one had to go to the kinds of studies which Dr. Sanford and

---

[1] New York: Doubleday, 1955; and compare my discussion in "Orbits of Tolerance, Interviewers and Elites," *Public Opinion Quarterly*, XX (1956), 49–73.

his colleagues have been doing at Vassar and to watch the way a two-step flow of influence occurs: from the faculty to the students, and then from student leaders to the general run of students, in which the students mediate what it is of the faculty they will accept.

Student restriction of output

Now—and this is very clear in the various studies—the faculty represents for the students, as do the upperclassmen, a somewhat upper middle-class (executive or professional) urbanity, including a general "tolerance." Business and professional life demand flexibility of young people, not doctrinal adherence, and the students decide in the college environment how much to "produce," much as the factory workers in a factory decide how much to produce.

To put it another way, just as in the factory productivity rises in spite of immense restrictions of production by workers, so the colleges get better, I think, in spite of the resistances students put up against being educated. Thus, I believe that if Dr. Jacob had done his study two decades earlier, he would have found even less emancipation in the colleges than at present. And to recur to my metaphor or analogy, colleges get better much in the same way that industry gets better, namely, that there is better management, better organization, better personnel guidance, better "tools," in terms of better texts, better readings, more penetrating examinations, and so on. But ratebusters are as much busted in the one situation as in the other, and enthusiasm denigrated in both. To repeat, students are the ones who decide how much any one student can be allowed to produce without being thought a "square" or a ratebuster. But colleges differ very much in the degree to which they are dominated by a monolithic student culture or broken up into heterogeneous subcultures, and in the latter situation obviously there is not one group which is influential but a greater number and a greater chance for differentiated performance. Dr. Jacob touches on some of the factors which lead to variations in the weight of atmospheric pressures in one campus as against another.

Thus, one of the most interesting studies he mentioned is one done by Samuel Stouffer and Jackson Toby, a study of student norms at Harvard.[2] This study presented students with an hypothetical conflict between telling or not telling on their friends whom they had seen cheat in an examination in situations where the former either would or would not be punished by the authorities, and a surprising proportion of around 40 percent of the students would "let their friends down" if they endangered their own records by conniving with them. That is, if they wouldn't be found out, the students would not tell on their friends but, if they would be found out, they would tell. The implication I draw from this is that at Harvard there is little solidarity among students as a group, even among students who might use the term "friend" as labels for one another, and that to the degree that one can draw conclusions from such a "projective" experiment, ratebusters among the students at Harvard would not be punished. Conceivably this is related to Professor Jacob's finding about Harvard, namely, that there is a great deal of autonomy there. And some aspects of this autonomy may be less amiable than other aspects!

Buffers between students and faculty (and other elders)

To return to the more common pattern of the youth defending themselves against their elders and against being influenced or touched by what happens in college—this defense is a sign of their guardedness today, their fear of being "sold." And yet, as I have said, there is emancipation in the colleges as compared with the general population, and one must ask, what are the factors responsible for this relative emancipation?

If you compared your students, Dr. Jacob, with nonstudents, if one could find nonstudents of similar socioeconomic position, one would find the former more emancipated. One reason for this, I suggest, is that there is greater heterogeneity in most colleges—and therefore greater opportunities for tolerance to develop—than there is in the suburban high schools. But I must

[2] Stouffer and Toby, "Role Conflict and Personality," *American Journal of Sociology*, LVI (1941), 395–406; see also Stouffer, "Analysis of Conflicting Social Norms," *American Sociological Review*, XIV (1949), 707–17.

qualify this by pointing out that in many colleges students protect themselves against the threat of heterogeneity through joining the "suburb" of the sorority and fraternity, and conversely in some of the better suburban high schools there is more pressure for mixing, for tolerance, than there is in many fraternity-dominated colleges. Beyond that, activities, of course, mix people; that is, the students who go out for the campus paper or the student council are likely to have wider horizons than the average student and, while as a result they may be quite alienated and considered eccentric or unrepresentative, they may nevertheless have some influence in getting the students at large to be less resistant to the values represented by the faculty. Indeed, much the same thing happens among the faculty members, namely, that the leaders among the professoriate represent more liberal views—views Professor Jacob would find sympathetic—than the general run of *academia*. There is evidence for this in the forthcoming study of the attitudes of social scientists toward academic freedom, a study undertaken by Professor Paul Lazarsfeld and sponsored by the Fund for the Republic.[3] His tables show that at the leading colleges the most influential and "productive" professors are the most likely to vote for Stevenson and to hold views which make their presidents shudder or give the presidents cause for trouble with their alumni and other off-campus groups. But the other less-gifted men, or men less productive in whatever measure one uses, in these institutions are more liberal than they would be were they teaching at less liberal institutions. In other words, if we compare men of similar background and education and relative lack of distinction at leading institutions where the climate is liberal and at middle-level institutions where the climate is conservative, their own outlook will reflect that of the opinion leaders on their campus. The Bennington study of Theodore Newcomb and the various studies of Nevitt Sanford indicate much the same phenomenon.[4] (There are very interesting exceptions.

[3] Paul F. Lazarsfeld and Wagner Thielens, Jr., *The Academic Mind: Social Scientists in a Time of Crisis* (Glencoe, Ill.: Free Press, 1958).

[4] On the Bennington study see Newcomb, *Social Change and Personality* (2nd ed.; New York: Dryden Press, 1958); on the Vassar studies, see Nevitt Sanford, Mervin D. Freedman, *et al.*, "Personality in the College Years," *Journal of Social Issues*, XI (1956), 1–70.

At U.C.L.A., for instance, the college paper is distinctly illiberal. Maybe that is Los Angeles; I don't know what it is.[5])

So far I have not said anything, save by implication, concerning the parental culture and its bearing on the student. If the student attends a college in his home community, and perhaps especially if it is thought of as a "community college," he may remain closer to the orbit of his parents' views not only because he is still living at home but also because the college itself doesn't seem too different from high school. However, in general, the student in college mediates between his parental culture and his peer culture. He doesn't tell his family on the whole about his roommate's sexual or drinking activities. If he does, he underplays it. Nor does he tell the family about the professor's view on the United Nations. He plays it cagey and "cool" and avoids controversy in this situation.

Yet I feel uncomfortable as soon as I have referred to the students as cool and cagey. In this connection I want to second what Dr. Killian said a moment ago about the "ethnocentric" accusations our generation levels against young people, in which we interpret the behavior of young people in the light of our own nostalgia and therefore often block cross-generational communication. Not only do students mediate faculty views in talking to their parents, but in talking to us as faculty members, they may too readily accept our own perceptions of their situation. Indeed, one of the things which is most striking about today's young people is that they do accept so readily many of the unpleasant things said about them by our generation. Perhaps their acceptance and acquiescence are illustrated by their willingness to confirm the prophecies of doom which are made about them!

As we all realize, one of the phenomena responsible for this cross-generational gap is that the students of today are being taught by men of the 1930's who had different idealisms, and therefore now call the young "materialistic." But the motives of the young, as Dr. Killian said, are opaque. This is partly their guardedness. They fear closeness with their teachers in some all-

---

[5] Since the meeting, I have been told that the student paper at U.C.L.A. was "purged" by the administration and that its later reactionary tone reflects that experience.

male settings; they fear closeness with each other. (I think that is a part of the situation at Harvard, which may help explain why so many would let their friends down.) One of the reasons that they are guarded with their teachers is again paradoxical, in my judgment, and that is that the teachers are seldom the pedants or ham actors who were teaching in the 1920's, but much better. This very improvement, however, has some ambiguous consequences. The better a teacher is, the more a student may fear to be influenced by him. The students of today are more serious than in an earlier generation but their very willingness to study creates problems for them of feeling overawed by teachers who are very erudite, who have read many books, and who sometimes write for little magazines.

Since teachers are better, they make more demands and students can less easily disregard the curriculum. The students are working at General Electric, as it were, under the supervision of high-grade time-study people, that is, with more subtle supervision than in the case of the old benevolent, but sometimes indolent or unsophisticated, despots of an earlier tycoon era (in which, of course, there were tycoons in *academia* as well as outside of it).

The altered character of student idealism

However, I don't believe it is right to say that the students are materialistic (nor is it right to say they are idealistic). They are certainly not mad for possessions. There isn't much possibility that a member of today's student generation will either build or buy a large estate as a showplace. They want salaries which are modest, on the whole, in order to support not splendor but the good life, and they don't know how much the good life costs: that is one reason their demands are modest. They are not gadget-happy. That is, their materialism, as it is described in the Jacob report, is not the materialism of the noncollege person, who is terribly pleased to have the consumer goods which his strata were previously denied.

But such idealism as they have is not the idealism of an older generation. That is, it is not political; it is, however, often civic, and I think this is a distinction which perhaps Dr. Jacob would like to comment on, for he speaks of the young as in some ways self-centered. But the "self," in my opinion, is not the individual self; it is a series of concentric circles which include, in the first place, the family. The young people of today are, above all, family idealists in the sense that, far more than in an earlier, more career-minded and more plainly "selfish" age, they are devoted to their spouses and their children.[6] And the family reaches out into the neighborhood, which is a manageable "extended family," rather than into larger political affairs, which they believe have either been solved by our generation or rendered insoluble by our generation.

This ideal of "togetherness," whatever its limitations, does have one positive aspect which Dr. Jacob underplays, namely, that many young college people (not all, of course) don't want invidious distinctions of race or class, and this isn't only "tolerance," but an actual code of personal conduct. That is, the young people in many good colleges today, while they are not going to fight city hall, may fight to elect a Negro if he runs for class office. The students will, in their personal lives, resist and resent any of the standard old-line bigotries. And I think this widespread phenomenon at better institutions goes beyond "tolerance," because it is not tolerance for the bigotry of fellow students.

Also, in their personal lives there is a decline of the rating-dating kind of phenomenon in relation to the opposite sex, in which one counts how many scalps one can find; there is, rather, a search for a more companionable or mature or monogamous (though not puritanical) relationship.

Above all, the idealism of the young in this very guarded and, how should I say, covert way in which nobody could possibly be allowed to suspect them of any enthusiasm, shows up in various searches for the meaning of life, private life, but still meaning, whether in a new-found interest in religion or in courses in sociology and psychology, in which this search is often frustrated

---

[6] The college graduate of an earlier day was, of course, also devoted to his family in the sense of wanting very much to be a good provider and, at times, in Veblenian terms to have them capably represent the family's social and economic attainments. But today the family is seen primarily as a source of responsiveness and companionship, and much less as a vehicle for inheritance of property and name.

by the faculty. In sum, the students tend to underplay their own idealism because it doesn't fit traditional forms, and thus they "confirm" our somewhat misleading image of them. Though their devotions are private not public, they have more of them than they would like to let on.

Complexities of impact

Now I want to turn to certain problems of measurement implicit in what I have said; namely, how does one discover the quality of a climate or series of climates on a campus and how does one measure the impact of the faculty? These are questions on which the Jacob report is illuminating. Indeed I might say that in one respect the Jacob report is endearing for, having sat among my colleagues in general education at Chicago now for many years, and having heard them say that one particular program would be fatal and another would solve all problems, it is something of a relief to realize that no book or program makes very much difference! And that colleges, in order to be different, must be markedly so. The standard academic trivia for "marginal differentiation" have no importance. One could put it this way: a college must say to the student, and it doesn't matter what form the statement takes: "This is not high school any more; this is different!"

As students have become more mature, they expect comparably more in college. They find, although there is more than there was, it is comparably less than they expected, and therefore it seems like high school. High school could be called an ersatz college, if you like; that is, it has a quasi sophistication of its own (including an increasing number of courses in social studies). One result is that when Dr. Jacob looks to see what the impact is of a particular course, he finds that in the same college the control group which hasn't had the course is not different from the students who have. (That is, Professor Jacob examines studies which compare the outlook or values of students who have been exposed to a particular course and those who have not; and many of these studies demonstrate that the course has no effect except to convey information.) However, if the general social environment has, in effect, exposed everyone to the ideas of the course, if those ideas have filtered down from those who have taken the course, then we would expect this result. Judging from our experience at the University of Chicago, I would say this procedure leaves open, as I am sure Professor Jacob would agree, an important question; namely, what is the "critical mass" of the college: how many students in what positions of influence have to take a course before everyone in effect takes it? You know the famous remark that was in the *New Yorker*. Somebody was asked if he had read such-and-such a Book-of-the-Month Club book, and the person answered, "Not personally." Well, there are a lot of people in the better colleges who haven't taken the course personally, and yet they have been exposed to a set of ideas. I think one can illustrate such a phenomenon at a place like Antioch where the ideas and values of the faculty have a strong impact on the students despite the fact that there is no large-scale general education program or other coherent or unified curricular core. In other words, I suggest that Antioch creates or reinforces a student culture which is based partly on the work program but which also absorbs ideas taught in courses which not everyone takes (certainly, the Wesleyan studies show the success of the Antioch graduate when he continues in scholarship and science). Thus, the question remains: How many students and what sorts of students have to be exposed to what encounters, in order to get a critical mass which will ignite the general community of students? To what extent must there be a common culture and how wide must this culture reach? And to what extent, if it doesn't reach to the total campus, can it create subcultures within the campus?

The studies which Dr. Jacob relies on have mostly been done by psychologists. They compare control groups which are classroom groups, or are classes, rather than what you might call sociometric groups or "natural" groups. There is a good deal of research currently under way on the flow of influence in the medical profession which shows which doctors first adopt new drugs; and these studies show that the doctors who are well integrated into groups are most likely to adopt new drugs, because they are protected by the group from kickbacks if they don't work; and if one looks at the structure of the groups which do adopt innovations, one finds that the leader is usually the well-integrated colleague of a leading medical man who is told by others, "Why don't you try out the new wonder drug?" and who, if he does successfully try it out, will then disperse it to the rest of the group.[7] Similarly, at Vassar, the group that Dr. Sanford leads is attempting to trace these subgroups which are opinion leaders in the college climates by describing subtypes and by treating each year's class as a group, as well as differentiating among students in terms of social background, that is, whether they went to prep school, and so on. I am inclined to think that only this type of "anthropological," subcultural investigation, when combined with psychological studies, will reveal how the students mediate faculty influence and impact.

Monolithic and diverse climates

Correspondingly, one of my colleagues at Chicago, James S. Coleman, a sociologist, has been doing a study of high schools to compare high schools in which there is only one road to success —let us say, for the boys, athletics (and being "good guys," too), and for the girls, being attractive and dated by athletes—with those high schools in which there are many roads to success. (Incidentally such heterogeneity includes the possibility that there is a sufficient group to support a delinquent culture, as well as other subcultures of which we would approve.) His work indicates, as one might expect, that size has a lot to do with it; indeed the concept of "critical mass" I have been employing comes from him. Without a large and heterogeneous student body, the individual's own heterogeneous qualities, of which he is not even aware or of which he represses awareness, may not find support and nutriment among his peers. Moreover, there has to be some faculty or communal support for the minority groups. Coleman has been looking at yearbooks of high schools to see how wide can be the differences among high schools in similar socioeconomic environments in what they regard as "ability." The yearbooks

[7] Compare James S. Coleman, Herbert Menzel, and Elihu Katz, "The Diffusion of an Innovation among Physicians," *Sociometry*, XX (1957), 253–70; and see also Elihu Katz and Paul F. Lazarsfeld, *Personal Influence* (Glencoe, Ill.: Free Press, 1955).

indicate what students have accomplished and thereby what is defined as an "accomplishment" as well as how widely spread among students different accomplishments are. There are high schools in which there is a monopoly of what is defined as an accomplishment so that students who are prominent in one activity are also prominent in others, while the majority of students are, so far as the yearbook reveals, prominent in nothing. In contrast, other schools have wider reaches of what is defined as a relevant activity, or they may simply democratize without redefining talent. And these differences are to be found while holding constant such matters as the socioeconomic level of the parents, or the tax base of the school, or the proportion of students who go on to college, and so on.

In one school, for instance, almost everyone, whatever else he is, whether he be an athlete or a "brain," is also involved in some musical activity, because the school, as at Joliet, has had a long tradition of musical activities. This can be traced back to zealous and pioneering people on the faculty. Indeed, one devoted person, caring deeply about music, and winning the devotion of both the students and the community for it, can over a long period of time alter the potential roads to success and esteem in the school and, hence, its total climate.

Ambivalence in faculty-student relations

Such considerations bring me to a question which I am sure Dr. Jacob meant to raise, at least by implication, namely, whether professors really want to have an impact on their students. The fact that professors deplore the lack of impact that they have should not, of course, persuade us to take them at their word, since the results Dr. Jacob found may conceivably be those which are unconsciously desired by at least a large segment of the faculty. There are, of course, many colleges where nothing the faculty could do could possibly change things, so entrenched is the student culture and so weak and ineffective the faculty culture. But at institutions of better quality I have had the experience over and over of hearing the students disparaged by the faculty and then of discovering, through talking with students, and reading their newspaper and literary magazine, that the students didn't quite deserve the opinion the faculty held of them. That opinion might serve the purpose *inter alia* of justifying the faculty's lack of concern with them. The attitude of the faculty is ambivalent. They wish, in a way, to have an audience among students, but this is not the audience that advances them professionally; and the result often is that they let down that potential minority among the students who would look to them for leadership, precisely because it is a minority. There isn't time to go into the converse matter—namely, the students who, for unconscious reasons of their own, encourage the faculty to form a depressed estimate of them, and, hence, to demand less of them in the way of commitment.

And I need not tell this group assembled here that careers in *academia* depend on the ability to leave a particular college community, so that the cosmopolitanism of a school which emancipates its students to some extent is bought at the price of non-captivity of its faculty.

But I think there is something else—and certainly here one would have to go into detail on particular fields of study which differ in this respect: In general, I suppose, one could use Yeats' phrase, "the best lack all conviction," and say that the students who come to college with openness and enthusiasm find themselves up against gamesmen, both among fellow students and the faculty. I know college professors in the humanities who like to get a student to read a "sophomoric" book and, when the student falls for the book, attack it and, thus, the student. Similarly, they will take poetry that they consider corny and assign it, allow the students to commit themselves, and then deride them. So, too, I think one can find a good many examples of this among social scientists, where it may take the form of deriding do-gooders.

Now, when the university and college administrations realize this or read the Jacob report or the Sanford and Freedman report on Vassar, they are likely to jump to the conclusion that the college teachers whom one really ought to get are those who care primarily about their students, rather than about their subject matter or about the esteem in which they are held among fellow scholars. But I think most of us here recognize that this is no adequate solution. It is not even an undiluted blessing for the students to be taught by men who are primarily preoccupied with them; rather, such professors can be a little like those mothers who are overdevoted to their children, spending all their time at home with them rather than following their own interests or a career, being frustrated as a result, and perhaps too possessive. There has to be at least a double audience for faculty members, of students and of colleagues; if students are their only audience, they are as likely to endanger their students as to help them.

A generation of gamesmen?

I must confess that there are times when I get so depressed about the dilemmas I have been describing, whether at the high school or at the college level (at the graduate level, I think matters are even worse in some fields and that students get stupider, narrower, as they move on to graduate study), that I am driven to feel that nothing of real value, nothing deeply involving the students' own values, should be taught in college because it will become tainted there by gamesmanship. That is, everything of importance should be extracurricular, because, if you have as a faculty a generation of gamesmen, the students are going to find that the very best subjects are the most dangerous ones because they are led on by these bright, but unconvinced, men who are erudite, but poor specimens of mankind; and the students would be better off if they were being taught relatively routine subjects without trifling in class with things that really matter, and were, meanwhile, to discover that what really matters are their own outside activities, whether in drama, music, the student paper on writing, or other things.

This is when I really get depressed. When I am only moderately depressed, I think this is obviously not a sufficient disposition of the problem. Among many other reasons, it is insufficient because the problems that are revealed in the Jacob report arise when many of the important and value-laden topics cannot any longer be left to extracurricular discovery by excited and adventurous students working on their own. This is occurring because the general culture is moving very fast to catch up with whatever the academy does in the humanities and the social sciences;

indeed, television, *Life* magazine, paperbooks, and such, dis-
seminate leading ideas rapidly, with the result that the "shock of
recognition" in attending college is greatly attenuated.   It is
this very dissemination which creates some of the problems discussed in the Jacob report.   Hence, one cannot avoid teaching
important subjects; the students have already been exposed to
them.   One has to go beyond the sound barrier, so to speak, and
do better, no matter what it takes in the way of energy and cour-
age to do better.

And to do better means, then, not using the clichés Dr. Killian
spoke of at the outset to justify confinement by one's academic
discipline.   One has to make contact with student values and
take the risks involved.

The context of a teacher's impact

I want to take another example from the Coleman high school
study.   It is a good example.   One of the things Coleman did
was compare different Illinois and Kansas City high schools that
sent many high school students to college with those that did
not to try to see some of the factors involved in sending students
to college.   Of course, family background and socioeconomic
position are important, but Coleman was interested in the factors
that the school itself might influence, apart from a fortunate or
underprivileged setting.   And he found one school in an industrial
area (where the industry helps provide a tax base), a school which
sent on to college and to good colleges a surprising number of
students who became scientists.   When he visited the school to
try to understand its accomplishment, he discovered a biology
teacher, a well-trained man who happened to land at this school
where he had become the wrestling coach.   He had never wrestled
in his life.   The school has a Polish and Czech constituency.   These
are very stocky boys; they aren't big enough for either football or
basketball; they are not miners' sons but steel workers' sons.   The
school has won all the wrestling championships in the State of
Illinois.   Since the coach is also the biology teacher, he sends some
of the best wrestlers on to the University of Chicago, and they
become biologists and doctors.

There may seem to be a contradiction between what I said

earlier concerning the overdevoted parent or teacher and my example of this biology teacher who cared enough about his students and his relations with them to learn how to teach wrestling. To some extent, the contradiction can be reconciled by making clear that it is not a question of the teacher's spending all his time with the students but rather a question of the intensity or aliveness of the contacts with them that he does have.

Beyond that, he must be willing to take the risks of disorienting the student and hence facing his hostility and resentment. Thus, it is clear from Sanford's work at Vassar that that college is prepared to disorient freshmen. Colleges have always disoriented students, but it has become harder to do this in our day because we can no longer be as innocent about our casualties or as blind about the harm we may do. Dr. Killian and I have discussed this with Dr. Dana Farnsworth, who can give grim report on the disorientation that the very excellences of a college can produce. Our knowledge tends to make us, in Dr. Jacob's words, psychiatric babysitters for the students; we cannot help becoming that and we should do so; that is, we must provide the ancillary services of support and counseling to make up for our own deficiencies, while continuing to take the risks of disorienting students.

We also have to be clear about our own values if we want to change student values, and clear about what we want for our students; and we have to be quite convinced that what we want is not to prepare them for life-as-given nor for most of the going models of the academician. No less important, we have to be willing to redefine what our academic cultures have previously called ability or talent, because one of the ways in which we can contaminate our relations with students is through grades, which serve the same purpose in the academic system that money does in the social system, that is, of avoiding questions of meaning.

A *"consumer research institute"* for higher education

Let me now very briefly mention several things which I think could be done by a group such as this, or other such groups, which might have immediate consequences for the problems Dr. Jacob raises. Of these, one of the most important—and I think that Dr. Killian won't mind if I expound this (he has heard me before)—is better consumer research and publications about colleges. I would like to see as much attention devoted to consumer research in higher education as we now devote to consumer research in commodities. No FTC censors college public relations releases. No pure food and drug law controls what development officers say. And the result is that students are not always brought to the school in which they can profit most, given their characteristics, from education.

It is my impression that the Amherst program is not widely known among academic people and not known at all among guidance people in most high schools, with the result that Amherst is not differentiated by its constituency from other Ivy League colleges. It might as well be Bowdoin or Williams, as far as many know, and although Amherst gets more applicants than it can take, there are not enough interesting applicants who could profit from this interesting program. Two things result. The best faculty members will not stay because they will go to places where students will match the program, and students go there who should go somewhere else.

And the situation is the same at the other colleges for other reasons. Often a college has declined, but the students do not know it yet; and there is not sufficient "feedback" from educational experiments on one side and there is inertia on the other. And I would like to know how many college guidance people are going to use the Jacob report in advising students.[8] For instance, Jacob talks about authoritarian-minded students and the kind of place to which they should go to profit most from their own devices and defenses, and this is not, of course, something taken into account by guidance people on the whole.

Experimental colleges

Along the same line, there should be more satellite colleges or colleges within colleges, such as has been tentatively at least thought about at Vassar, where new things could be tried out with the support of established institutions and where the uniformity

---

[8] For that matter, faculty members also need consumer research on institutions, for they are frequently misguided in moving or in thinking about moving from one institution to another.

of climate at large institutions could be broken up. Thus, one can create diversity *within* institutions in spite of the fact that sufficient diversity *among* institutions is not a very common phenomenon.[9] And this applies to curricular as well as to extra-curricular activities.

The cultural content of learning

Then a point relevant perhaps only for Ivy League schools: I am convinced that one of the reasons the faculty has so little impact in the Ivy League institutions is that the faculty and students characteristically compose what some students of the Latin American countries, notably Erich Fromm, call a "male-vanity culture." [10] The male-vanity culture is such that the men are so vain they cannot learn, for they should know everything already. One of the ways to do something about a male-vanity culture is to introduce women on the faculty, if not in the student body. In the all-male colleges, I should like to see more women on the faculties, and I think they would have an impact because, as I have suggested, I believe that some of the guardedness on both sides is due to the fear of homosexuality.

This is a hypothesis; I am not sure about it. To examine such questions there should be a closer connection between the academic faculty and the people in the clinic. At present what the clinic learns about the casualties created by the academic people is often misinterpreted. Let us say a person in the clinic, a psychiatrist, gets a student who has a learning block. He isn't likely to understand how complex the academic culture is and how it might have a hand in creating that block. So he tells the student, "You have an Oedipus complex. You have to get rid of your hostility to your father," which is a familistic explanation of a more

[9] As everyone knows, there is immense diversity among institutions at the various levels of American higher education—and some of the varieties are described in my book *Constraint and Variety in American Education* (Lincoln, Neb.: University of Nebraska Press, 1956)—but I was referring here to diversity among leading institutions which emphasize the liberal arts and maintain relatively high academic standards; there is instead a standardization of program, which means that if one can find a course at one of these institutions, one can almost surely find it at all the others.

[10] In a seminar in the Yale Anthropology Department with the late Ralph Linton and Carl Withers in 1949.

complex and partly cultural phenomenon. Conversely, the academic people can go merrily on creating the casualties without getting any repercussions from them, and often feeling superior to the psychotherapist.

College and initiation

But above all, as I have said, a clear break from high schools seems to me the great need, however that can be achieved, so that the student feels that something earthshaking should happen here, that the old rules do not hold. To repeat, it gets harder and harder to do this as the general culture (even including the high school culture, however the university professors may look down on it) catches up with us. Thus, at one of the leading prep schools last year there was a first-rate course given in American civilization by a man who had studied with Oscar Handlin at Harvard, and I wonder whether the boy coming out of that course or out of similarly high-powered preparation is going to find college really new and exciting.

We cannot say to the high school, please don't anticipate us, any more than we can say it to television and other media or to the parents who more and more are themselves among the college-educated; and, therefore, the demands put on the colleges today for superlative quality are ever so much greater than most of us, I think, recognize. And Dr. Jacob's findings indicate that, in the general emancipation of the college-bound, the colleges themselves create no new initiation and do not take advantage of what is really an opportunity.

Discussion

Individual versus group responsibility

Mr. Clark Kerr: I should like to ask about one phenomenon to see how you explain it. This grows out of the Berkeley experience with a panty raid some time ago. In the 1930's, out of which many of us come, when the students undertook something outside, it tended to be an individual prank. The problems we have at Berkeley, and apparently at some other places around the

country, tend not to be with individual pranks but with a kind
of mass disorder—the trouble tends to come in a mass situation,
rather than from the ideas of individual students or small groups.
What are your observations on this?

MR. RIESMAN: Don't you think this has something to do with
the greater maturity and worldliness of the young, so they dare
not be foolish alone and can only be foolish together? Indeed,
I often have the feeling that panty raids are an attack on the professors of the thirties. They are almost saying, "Well, we can
be rash, too."

I don't know if this would be true at Berkeley, but at some
places I have suspected that students hear our verdict and have
read our commentaries on them, and they want to show us that
"We aren't so sane and safe as you think—look what we did."

MR. KERR: They do it in crowds of thousands at a time and
if there is any question of even minor penalties, the argument
of some of the students and some of the people close to them
will be, "Yes, but we were not responsible. We were doing it as
part of a large group."

So it isn't a kind of rebellion with willingness to take the
consequences. It is rather an attitude of "I wasn't responsible for
what I did. I did it with a large number of people. I did it with
my peer group, and I am not personally responsible for my action.
And therefore I should not be held punishable in any way."

CHAIRMAN KILLIAN: There is another kind of interesting phenomenon, a rebellion against authority, which I think is grow-
ingly characteristic of American student bodies and which may
be a very healthy situation. It seems to be an unwillingness to
accept anything if a faculty or administration or an institution
says it ought to be. And it seems also to be a terrific preoccupation with the feeling that students must be treated as adults,
that they are no longer high school students and they resent
being treated as such. They object often to any kind of rule or
regimentation or even orderly process. As I say, this may be
very healthy, but it runs counter to some of the things you have
been saying.

MR. KERR: Would you say that they object as individuals or as groups? My short experience at Berkeley has been that, as individuals, it is almost terrifyingly easy to handle them.

Mr. Riesman: Have you read Freidson's report on student government, which shows how easy it is to manage student government?

Chairman Killian: But another thing one sees is a lack of willingness on the part of students to respond to student government.

Mr. Riesman: Maybe we can sort something out here. The students, as I have said, fear to be "had"; they fear to be "suckers"; they are afraid of authority, because it might lead them into situations which would alienate them from the group, which would ask them in some way or other, to be ratebusters, as student government, in effect, often does.

That doesn't seem to me to be the same as being antiauthoritarian in attitude. If you are talking about parietal regulations, then I would say that students are mature today, they are more mature and steadier than they used to be. You have to put your experience of the panty raids down against the fact that students conduct their relations with each other with much more sagacity and maturity. They are steadier as drivers, as dates, and in many ways as students. As I have said, students are intolerant of any bigotries. There is no aristocracy among them. They don't reject the hoodlum. They prefer to amalgamate with the "hoods" rather than with the elite, and you might call this the dishonor system instead of the honor system, so that certain infiltration from below is part of their democracy. This is where the tolerance comes in. It is tolerance for the lower; it is not tolerance for the aristocrat.

The high school–college break

Chairman Killian: May I ask a loaded question? Do you feel that highly selective colleges which have residential systems are moving toward an absence of parietal rules and that parietal rules represent the unwillingness to break with the high school atmosphere, which you think is so important, and that thus we have a continuation of the parental kind of discipline?

MR. RIESMAN: I would say that this is true, wouldn't you, in fact, if not in theory?

RAYMOND F. HOWES: May I ask a question on the need for the great break between high school and college? We seem to be well advanced in an era in which a larger number of our students are going to transfer from junior colleges into four-year colleges. That presumably means they get two breaks, each of which is less than the one break from high school to the four-year college, particularly because the junior college may very well be in the community where the student lives. Is that going to be an academic disaster to whole generations of students in the future?

MR. RIESMAN: I think so. Not to put it into too dramatic a framework, I think no one should be allowed to go to college less than five hundred miles from home without good reason.

CHAIRMAN KILLIAN: Your feeling is that this simply continues the parental or the high school environment, and doesn't cause a dramatic, effective break?

MR. RIESMAN: This is, of course, especially true when the community college, as is so often the case, is under the control of the local high school and is even in the same building.

MR. KERR: May I ask an unpleasant question: whether college isn't going to become more like high school for the vast majority of students in the United States, as greater numbers go into junior colleges and state colleges, and whether the break may not have to come at the time they enter graduate work, if it comes at all?

MR. RIESMAN: This is implicit in all you say. Wouldn't you say another reason for consumer research is that one ought to encourage transfers? What happens, I suppose, is that a few dedicated people in the junior college say to the most gifted students, "Get out of here. Go somewhere else after a year or two." The others need for their own salvation to keep the few good ones there, just as the University of Chicago found in its effort to get students in the eleventh and twelfth grades that the school principals wanted to keep around the ones who were running the student paper and student government.

Consumer research on colleges

CHAIRMAN KILLIAN: How do you think we can accomplish consumer research that reveals the quality of institutions? It will never come from the academic community.

MR. RIESMAN: It requires a respectable group with large foundation support to be that courageous. It is fantastic that decisions which are relatively trivial are protected by law. We have consumer research when the dimensions of decision are minute—research about cars, about housewives and their preference for one or another shape of soap, about teen-agers and the bottle shapes they prefer for Coca-Cola. Far more critical decisions about college choice are made by chance, by convention, by high school guidance counselors, and by all kinds of high school prestige factors which operate to subordinate the youngster to the interests of the high school. I don't know the answer to the question of how such research could be done, but I think it is the most important single thing which could be done. For instance, just to publish the College Board scores or the Graduate Record Area Examination scores of colleges would be salutary.

CHAIRMAN KILLIAN: You mean, to publish the real facts about the small degree of selectivity that exists despite all we hear about high degree of selectivity?

MR. RIESMAN: That is right. This consumer research would have to be much better and more imaginative than commodity research, because of the different talents of young people and the need for matching talents and colleges. We could have freed many people from their parents' colleges better than admissions officers are now able to do, because such research would show the disaster for young people in going to what is for them the wrong college. We might fulfill much of the same kind of function in this respect that vocational guidance now fulfills in freeing young people from parental career decisions for them.

I simply cannot imagine anything which would aerate better the present situation than consumer research, or any time when it could be better afforded than now when the colleges are, on the whole, full anyway. So very few of them will go broke as a result. It would also be enormously useful for the faculty. I don't know whether the college presidents who are here have the same impression that I do. A faculty member in search of an institution is as misguided as the student. He doesn't know what the climate is like, even if he is a sociologist. He goes on the basis of hearsay and the repute of the college and whether it has a football team to his liking, without knowing which school provides the best opportunity for his development and his visit is not designed to show him the answer to that question. So he would greatly profit by this. Foundations would profit. In fact, I think foundations now do the best of consumer research, but they don't dare live up to this achievement in other kinds of research.

CHAIRMAN KILLIAN: I'd like to come back to the break between high school and college. There is another characteristic of students that some of us think we observe, and that is a great hesitancy to be on their own in matters of curriculum. Honors programs and other kinds of efforts to free the students from the normal routine are looked upon with great skepticism and fear. This is in part because of the grading system, because students think that unless they take all of the program and go through the whole process, it will affect their grades or their relative standing. It is very difficult to get students to break free and go on their own. The projection of the high school attitude is pronounced.

MR. RIESMAN: You are right. We saw some of that, didn't we, Miss Goddard, in our discussion at Vassar?

MISS SARAH GODDARD: That was exactly what struck me most in your discussion. I am particularly interested in two points which have been made: the necessity of the break between secondary school and college and then the discussion of consumer research.

What has interested me most in the past four months is the number of students, not only Vassar students, who stay. The Sanford study is exactly what we should be able to read before we go to Yale or Harvard or anywhere else. Students do not want merely hours and hours of guidance, verbal guidance. They really want to know and to have available for their own reading the kind of material that comes from the consumer research we have talked about or from the findings of the Sanford study.

CHAIRMAN KILLIAN: Well, now, in order to get the total picture before us, may I call on Dr. Jacob to comment on Dr. Riesman's comments and to extend his own report or to elaborate on it in any way he thinks appropriate.

I might add that I know of no report appearing recently that has caused so much discussion and so much surprise in academic circles, although some of us are not quite sure why it should have caused so much surprise.   We have a feeling that it was an extraordinarily courageous document to publish at this particular juncture.

Student Capabilities for Liberal Education

PHILIP E. JACOB

I SHOULD LIKE to enter a disclaimer or two at the beginning. As a political science teacher, I felt a serious lack of expertise in handling much of the material pertinent to this study, especially data of a psychological nature.

Then, I should confess that I entered upon the study with a set of biases. These are not clearly stated in the report, partly because they were almost completely reversed by the findings. For instance, I was, and probably still remain, an advocate of liberal education and of certain types of general education. I believed in the worthwhileness of the teaching function, and despite the report, still do. I am convinced that certain values do emerge from the good teaching of some students, even though we cannot yet clearly discern and objectively demonstrate such results on a large scale. The persistence of these biases leads me to hope that some of the findings tentatively advanced in the report will be subjected to searching scrutiny and that more intensive research than has been possible so far will warrant much more optimistic conclusions. As a matter of fact, my major recommendation is for the extension of research on some of these questions.

This leads me to a third disclaimer. The study is not based upon new data specifically gathered for the purpose. It is built completely upon data collected in other studies. There is therefore nothing really new in the report. Perhaps in the next stage of research fresh data will give us more complete and penetrating information than was possible here. I am confident we shall learn much from the publication of more findings from the Vassar study and the Princeton study.

I have listened with very great appreciation to Professor Riesman's searching critique, and feel that the reservations he has suggested are extremely well taken. I look forward to reviewing the study carefully in the light of his comments.

The problem of standardization

To me, the problem of major significance which emerges from this look at the contemporary student generation and its values is the problem of standardization. Frankly, I was not prepared to find the degree of uniformity and homogeneity in student attitudes and beliefs which seems to be the case. The lack of differentiation of values among students, according to their economic and social background, came as a surprise. The lack of differentiation according to the region of the country in which they study or the type of institutions in which they are enrolled is also remarkable. Whether a college is private or public, church-affiliated or secular, seems to have little influence in shaping a different outlook on the part of a majority of students.

There is also considerable homogeneity of students within particular institutions. One might expect among a motley array of students coming to study at an institution of national coverage a wide variety of attitudes or values, just because so many different backgrounds would be represented. Yet even in such institutions, students appear far more alike than different.

I should make clear, however, that there is always a deviant group, in fact several deviant groups, coming to 10 percent, or maybe 20 percent or more, on nearly every attitude, and this group offers a very real challenge.

Still, if one starts with the proposition that the educator's function, or the teacher's function, is to teach *everyone*, and I confess that as a beginning teacher this was my aspiration and the aspiration still lingers, then the problem is a very difficult one. If the teacher's responsibility is to all thirty people in a class—not merely to the provocative five or six—the standardization of the 80 percent greatly confines his efforts.

Group values

A second problem pinpointed by the study is the self-centeredness of student values, on the one hand, and their group depend-

ence, on the other. I think your reservation is quite well taken,
Dr. Riesman, that the self-centeredness is of a different character
than that of the "robber barons." It is familistic. It is tied in
with partnership in a group with which a student is concerned.
Yet this group feeling is quite distinct from what one might call
a *public* sense. There is no genuine communal feeling, or concern
for the general well-being of a society on the part of the largest
number of students. Their primary impulse is to satisfy themselves. To secure such satisfaction in the world as they see it,
they follow the crowd. More precisely, they agree to govern
their lives by what others do, in order to gain acceptance with a
group which they think can furnish the personal satisfactions
they crave. This determines their relationship to their peers,
to their families, and to the country at large.

This pattern of values runs counter to many of the objectives
that some of us as teachers have set. One objective in the social
sciences, for instance, may be to encourage a sense of outgoing-
ness on the part of students. Or we may be concerned merely to
examine the phenomena of our society as a door to wider knowledge. Others might wish to develop individual autonomy on the
part of students, so they can think for themselves. In the pur-
suit of any of these objectives, we would have to move against
the grain in the prevalent pattern of student values which stresses
self-satisfaction through group conformity.

Personal and academic life

A third problem concerns the immediate relationship of the
students to the educational process. A hiatus, a very substantial
one, has opened between the academic educational process and
student life. There is a failure of communication between the
academic community and the students' own community.

I don't feel this is a failure to communicate ideas. I do agree
that the students seem to be getting better and better in an intellectual sense. They are able more and more to beat the academic game. Perhaps this accounts for the phenomenal rise in
the grade average at Yale and other places where we understand
the "dean's list" is no longer significant. But at that point communication seems to stop. Students learn what is necessary to

pass the examination and to meet the accepted campus scholastic standard. But then many of them move off into a separate world of existence, which the teacher is not invited to enter.

I was particularly impressed by a report from one of the best teachers I have witnessed in action. He told me that in three years at this institution, he had had only one occasion in which to see students in his home. And he said it would be the last because of the dismal results of his attempt. He extended an open, general invitation to his students to come to his home on a Sunday evening. Few but A students turned up. Then when he told them rather permissively, "This is your party, talk about anything you please," he found they were completely tongue-tied. They could not engage in a friendly, informal discussion. Finally, they got down to talking about sex and at that point the party thoroughly degenerated and people went away. There was never any inclination on their part or on his to renew the experience.

It seemed as though the instructor in effect had violated a kind of private world of the student. He had trespassed in a field which they considered theirs. They didn't want him around, and they didn't accept his invitation as a gesture of concern and personal interest. This seems to be characteristic at a good many places.

I am wondering whether this situation could be related to a hiatus *within* a good many students themselves, a hiatus between their intellectual life and other aspects of living; whether what we are witnessing is perhaps the developing of a clear separation between the mental process and the living process. Maybe the modern sophisticated student can handle living in two different worlds, unbothered by the necessity of integrating knowledge with decisions in his personal life.

Perhaps there is a further explanation of this hiatus, and here I would very much appreciate hearing Professor Sanford's views. I am impressed by some of the personality research that has been going on recently, which indicates that the hiatus in some people may be associated with a well-defined set of traits constituting a particularly dogmatic or rigid personality.

Apparently, it is very difficult for such people to appreciate an idea. And when they are invited to appreciate an idea, this disorganizes them, frustrates them, causes them no end of grief. An open invitation indeed makes it even more difficult for them to learn than if they are approached, to start with, with a fairly well structured and directed program or plan of consideration.

Perhaps this is enough of an annotation to the report.

Now, in regard to the implications for educational policy, stemming from the contemporary pattern of student values, I find myself very close indeed to the suggestions made by Dr. Riesman.

The mission of liberal education

A basic question is whether our conception of the mission of liberal education needs revision. I am sure some of us have had the feeling that this was a universal mission, one that should reach almost everybody. We have specifically advocated increasing the dose of liberal education for those who are going into the professions, and we have urged a substantial increase of the liberal element in the general requirements of the university and college curriculum. We have made the assumption that almost every individual can benefit from a liberal, general education.

But maybe this can no longer be assumed, considering the present nature of students who are coming to college and the point of view that they are bringing with them. Ought we to adopt the position that liberal education should be limited to those who can respond to it? Is this kind of higher education proper only for a segment of the student population and not for the great majority?

I find this distasteful to suggest because it seems to run counter to the humanistic concept that responsiveness to the "good" in life lies within the capacity of almost every person. I don't like to think that we are unable to make liberal education more widely effective. But if indeed we cannot make it effective for everyone, considering the limitations of faculty and the outlook and personality of many students, one alternative is to provide liberal education for, say, the 20 percent who are most responsive to it and content ourselves, for the remaining 80 percent, with a strict "tooling-up" for various vocations. This approach might be equally as applicable to students preparing for intellectual as for technical professions, to training a teacher of English as well as a mechanical engineer. In either case, college education would be essentially a tooling-up process accomplished largely by standardized instruction. It would also be quite economical, as I think there is enough evidence to show that such education can be about as effective when conducted in large groups as in small.

Individualized instruction

On the other hand, in liberal education, we could individualize instruction and diversify the programs to meet a wide variety of student differences. I have the feeling that if we standardize the liberal component of higher education, we simply confirm even more the standardization of values that seems to be occurring among students as a result of the social pressures they are experiencing. We shall only be able to break the mold of the standard pattern of values if we find active points of contact between the liberal education component and the particular student's problems and background.

Granted that this may be a dream impossible to realize, yet it represents a different point of departure than the prevalent tendency to stress a uniform general education curriculum for everyone. In this context, it might be worth considering whether it is possible to help individuals to live in two worlds at the same time. Maybe it is the job of higher liberal education to help the person make the adjustments that are necessary to keep the industrial system going and to find his place in it, and yet to have a private life that is creative and one which gives him satisfaction. If we think in terms of some such mission for liberal education, then we are confronted, if these data are valid, with a critical problem of communication between the academic institutions, the faculty in particular, and the students. How is that kind of mission to be fulfilled? I should like to know as a teacher.

The only suggestion I can offer for further exploration is the possibility of moving from an intellectually centered curriculum to an experientially centered curriculum.

There has been a tendency to concentrate more and more on book learning and less and less on the discovery of means by which students can actually partake of experiences that enable them to educate themselves. This hinders the maturing of personal values.

An alternative might be for an institution to grab the student firmly by the scruff of his neck and say, "These are the values that you shall hold." There are examples of institutions so organized that they have successfully broken through pre-existing student value patterns.

I am not at all sure, however, that that is compatible with the kind of goal for liberal education which we would espouse. Rather, some of us would hold that the self-cultivation of the student, the discovery of his own values through experience of one kind or another, is far more reliable and constructive in the long run. But how can such an unfolding of the self be achieved?

I have wondered whether a teacher in the liberal arts should not concentrate upon introducing as many situations of *discord* as possible into his students' experience. Perhaps the institution itself could build a student body which would have the germs of discord within it. A student might then have a chance to come smack up against another person who profoundly challenged the assumptions on which he had built his general pattern of values. Of course, today's student has developed a defense against this. I think his tolerance makes it extremely difficult for the technique of discord to work.

The importance of decision-making

Along another line, value-generating experience might include situations in which real decisions could be made by students within the framework of the subject they were studying, with consequences that they could witness.

Illustrations are hard to come by, because there simply isn't much of this kind of education going on. But maybe it would be possible to take a problem in political theory or in international organization and translate the problem out of the textbooks and the libraries into a concrete situation concerning which the student would be called on to find a definite solution, and have a chance to see his choice bear its repercussions.

So if we are thinking in terms of improving the process of communicating liberal values, perhaps investigation could proceed along this line of transforming an essentially intellectual experience into an intellectual experience plus. I do not mean to deprecate the intellectual side, but to add to it a base of actual student experience.

This leads me to a third suggestion. The United States National Student Association has made a real contribution in pointing out the long distance between the curriculum and what I believe we now call the "cocurriculum." It seems to me this gap is unfortunate. Perhaps greater potency in our educational processes would develop if the university or college itself took a major responsibility for the extracurricular life of the students, doing this, however, not in a dictatorial way.

In some situations, to be sure, an institution may need to adopt an imperative role in regard to such activities. I am thinking of campus organizations which are too strongly mold-setting. Perhaps the college should deliberately liquidate these. The students can hardly do it themselves. They are caught in a vicious circle, particularly in regard to fraternities. Firm administrative action may be necessary to break those shells which so enclose students when they come to the campus that the most independent of them do not achieve their independence.

With that exception, it seems to me the relationship between students, faculty, and administration should be one of cooperative endeavor to knit the cocurriculum into the curriculum, so that there can be a most intimate connection between the intellectual experience and the experience of campus life.

Finally, I couldn't agree more with Dr. Riesman on the need for guidance, measurement, and the whole gamut of activities devoted to trying to find out what it is that a student really has and where he can develop his potentialities most favorably.

Probably this process has to start well before college. But even if it hasn't been done adequately in the schools, colleges themselves should undertake a much more effective task of advising, encouraging reciprocal regard between student and faculty adviser, finding out what resources for growth the student has, and who, then, are the best instructors for his particular purposes. Perhaps he should even be asked to leave the university and go somewhere else.

Discussion

Social conformity as a goal

MR. KERR: What I am about to say now, I don't like. But I am going to say it anyway. We talk about the changing values of college students, and we do not like the direction in which they are changing. But maybe it is the attitude and values of the faculty members which ought to change. Granted that we have a great diversification of technical skills, still couldn't quite an argument be made that the fairly uniform social values and social skills of students today fit pretty well the world out of which they come and particularly the world into which they are going— the large corporation, the suburb, the mass trade union, and such?

And we might say they aren't as we were. Perhaps they aren't what we ideally would like to see them. They are not independent and individualistic, but they do fit the needs of our emerging industrial society. They are a kind of pre-Organization Man. I can just see, having done arbitration in the industrial scene, that the employers will love this generation, that they are not going to press very many grievances, there won't be much trouble, they are going to do their jobs, they are going to be easy to handle. There aren't going to be riots. There aren't going to be revolutions. There aren't going to be many strikes.

MR. RIESMAN: You mean only panty raids.

MR. KERR: Panty raids are not likely to exist in their later lives because they will live in suburbs and will be scattered. Maybe we ought to say that this is at least inevitable and perhaps, if we look upon our function as training people for society, that this is good. I don't like to admit the burden of my own argument. But let me simply put it on the table and ask whether we are not what is wrong rather than the current generation of students. Haven't they made a much better adjustment to this emerging industrial society with its large urban centers, mass organizations, than we have, and shouldn't we glory in their values rather than condemn them? Let me repeat that I dislike this idea.

MR. JACOB: I think it bears very directly on this question of re-evaluating the liberal part of education. Instead of the alternatives we have been considering, we might just accept culture adjustment as a premium product and forget about the value goals that we have normally associated with liberal education.

CHAIRMAN KILLIAN: I should like to ask Dr. Riesman if he feels that this concept of the degeneration of the Puritan ethic that Mr. Whyte has talked about and the development of the Organization Man is an inevitable process, the process toward conformity that goes with it, whether, therefore, the comment that Dr. Kerr has made is relevant or significant, and whether colleges are augmenting and furthering and making themselves a part of this changing process. I know this is a question that cannot be answered out of hand.

MR. RIESMAN: I am still thinking about Dr. Kerr's comments. I think what he ought to add to his picture, as one sees it very clearly and not entirely sardonically, is that the world into which young people are going is reasonably civilized. It is not so different from the academic world. My own feeling is that business and *academia* are becoming as organized as other previous social groupings, and this is the reason for making college different—it is not now different from enlightened business institutions which have their own educational programs.

MR. KERR: There is a degree of academic freedom in the corporation.

MR. RIESMAN: Yes, very much. If there weren't this tolerance and decency and civic-mindedness and academic-mindedness in the large corporation, our young people would have something to rebel against. The prices that they are asked to pay are all so subtle.

Putting into context what you said, Dr. Kerr, and what Dr. Jacob has just described as a homogenization process, there is a partial incorporation of good things by all institutional processes. So this problem of salvation by leaps becomes ever more difficult.

The danger of restricted productivity

I think there are at least two things which might be added and which are my answer to what Dr. Killian asked. The whole world "ain't" like that, but we are getting so different from the whole world that I no longer think productivity teams from other countries should come to study us. They should go to Japan or some other place. It all stems from the art of what I call conspicuous production. What I said before about disorientation, I really believe, because this life, I think, is only good for a certain mileage for the people themselves, and after the age of thirty-five or so, it shows its own built-in limitations in its meaninglessness and in that disaffection of people from it.

Let me put it another way. The restriction of productivity learned in college is continued until later. This is the greatest damage people can do to themselves in our society, never to allow themselves to care about their work.

This is what the younger generation misses, and it isn't quite made up for by the fact that they care about each other, because their caring about each other needs the variation or the dialectic of caring also about their work or something outside social relations, and this deprivation eventually takes its toll. Beyond that, I would answer that society has to be reorganized because the positive qualities I have just referred to—decency, civic-mindedness, a certain amount of freedom, a great deal of tolerance, and a minimum demand for conformity in any overt strait-jacket sense —these excellent qualities are not enough; they are quite consonant with the condition of anemia in human endeavor. One can see in the plateau of the "good life" which many Americans have attained that more is still necessary.

The college generation is being short-changed by being prepared for a life that lasts for only fifteen or twenty years; for the rest of their lives, they cannot see beyond the next step. Or if they can, they are genuinely upset.

HARRY D. GIDEONSE: A general conception that liberal education is compensatory to whatever the influences of society before the age of thirty-five are?

MR. RIESMAN: That is right.

MR. KERR: There is a certain logic to industrialization. It is a system that demands a certain amount of consistency, and people have to pay a certain price to get the benefits of industrial life. One of the prices they may have to pay and are apparently willing to pay is the price you have mentioned, and I would agree with your analysis.

Now, is it possible to have an industrial society, and in accord with the logic of industrialization, to encourage this greater freedom, and the deviant person, the deviant group, the rebel? Isn't it, rather, the logic of the industrial system that everybody depends on everybody else?

It is not only a question of going beyond the norm, which may cause trouble, too, but it is a question of falling below the norm which hurts everybody. That is the other aspect of the ethic, that you don't go above the norm, but you don't fall below it.

The way to sabotage the industrial system is to go too much away from the norm in either direction. Isn't one of the prices of the industrial system inherent in it, that we all have to fit into norms, and that we cannot have variety, and that life may therefore turn out to be less interesting? There will be better health, people will live longer, but it will be less interesting after age thirty-five. Isn't that the price we may have to pay?

MR. RIESMAN: To come back to the point about the students who don't take advantage of, and are rather frightened by, freedom, wouldn't you say that reactions of Americans to our own industrialization are exactly the same; that is, that we have now got it, that we can do it with one hand behind our backs, that the price paid in the periods of earlier industrialization is no longer a mortgage, even in the form of a national debt, that we, therefore, have the chance not to be run by it any more, not to be confined within it, and that we aren't because we have outrun the limits provided by the processes of industrialization?

HARALD C. BAKKEN: Let me make a comment to endorse enthusiastically the suggestion that Dr. Jacob makes with regard to experience-centered learning and to suggest an example in the very question of fraternities and sororities. It seems to me that on many campuses, where this has become a burning issue, it has provided exactly this kind of experience-centered training in which the student comes to grips in a way which directly affects him, with issues regarding democratic processes, regarding questions of democratic opportunities. This might serve as an example of the kind of experience-centered training which does provide, to some extent at least, for this integration of the student's personal life and his intellectual experience.

Weaknesses of selection by tests

CHAIRMAN KILLIAN: The whole process of selection for college, where there is a process of selection, has to do with objective tests which are of the verbal, the aptitude, or the mathematical kind. Is this likely to result in a degree of homogeneity in our student body because this is the factor we measure, rather than getting the other factors you describe? Isn't this a possible great fault that we are going to face and a great difficulty as the selective process increases in the years ahead? As far as I know, we have almost no techniques or measures or approaches for dealing with this kind of selective process.

MR. JACOB: Quite so. I feel that the development of more objective methods of understanding a student's personality is perhaps one of the most important contributions that could be made to resolve some of these problems. I suppose the interview is the only thing really that is widely practiced as a means of assessing personality.

CHAIRMAN KILLIAN: And widely variable in its effectiveness, almost capricious.

MR. RIESMAN: I don't think the situation is quite as you put it. I have discussed this with Frank Bowles, who agrees with my feeling, that with a long autobiography, such as Sarah Lawrence asks for, carefully read, and with some attention to the fact that the student may not have written it, with Rorschach tests, or other projective tests, one could do much better. But it would be more expensive, and his feeling is that the colleges are blocking the roads because the interview as a means of evaluation would expose them to the attack that it is less "objective" and also because it is more expensive and much more demanding of their facilities. So it isn't really that the instruments do not exist to do it.

MR. JACOB: Would there be some possibility that the problem

could be narrowed a bit by a six-month probation for students to which they come as if for a training program?

CHAIRMAN KILLIAN: This is a brutal way.

MR. JACOB: This at least might reduce the number of people from which one had to select. It would, of course, miss some people who might have come, but I cannot help feeling that we aren't doing enough even with the group that has already been admitted, inadequate though the standard of admission may be. The problem might be alleviated to some extent if there were in the freshman year a very much more intensive examination of students and guidance helpful to them.

MR. BAKKEN: Don't you have, in a sense, this kind of period, which is indicated by the large number of students who drop out during the first year, and isn't the problem that the basis on which they drop out or on which the selection during the first year is made is not wide enough. It is almost an exclusively academic one, or in some cases, a behavioral one, but largely academic, and you need to broaden the tools and techniques for this kind of selection.

JOSEPH C. McLAIN: I think there are an increasing number of high schools which are doing better and better analyses of their students through the tests and measurements that you have mentioned. Colleges should use these analyses and probably more attention and respect should be given to some of the things that are known by the schools.

I rebel a bit against the increased emphasis placed on College Board Aptitude Tests and that sort of objective testing. I think we can tell you a lot more about your students from our experience with them for several years than the verbal and the mathematics scores tell you.

Misgivings about Utopia

MR. HOWES: We seem to be moving in this discussion toward a Utopian situation, which would consist of two parts. First, you know everything you need to know about the student. Second, you know everything you need to know about the various institutions. Then you match them up. Nobody has said anything yet about what the cost might be for the individual student to go to the particular place with which he has been matched up in this sort of system.

My question is, suppose a very substantial number of the students who have been so analyzed and have been told, "You need to go to this institution or that institution in order to develop yourself fully," cannot go there for one reason or another. Is the additional frustration of knowing that when they go somewhere else, they are not in the right place, too big a price to pay for this?

W. MAX WISE: I think we are getting a bit afield in this discussion. My interpretation of Dr. Riesman's comments is simply that he hopes there will be some understanding, by people who help a student to choose a college, of what a given college might be able to do for him.

MR. RIESMAN: This problem of "feedback" and change within the single institution, even over a short period, cannot be handled, it seems to me, by the kind of generalization you speak of because the mobility of institutions, of faculty within institutions, of student climates within institutions, is so great and the turnover is so fast that one needs much more rapid assessment and reassessment of what is happening than I see any chance of at the present.

MR. WISE: There are so many variables in what students get from an institution. Sometimes the most improbable students get a great deal from an institution.

MR. KERR: Suppose you should have all this consumer information, wouldn't you want to mismatch the people, if you want to make them individuals?

DOUGLAS M. KNIGHT: We are trying to do the very thing that we claim undergraduates are doing. We are trying to make life uniform and easy.

CHAIRMAN KILLIAN: Perhaps, at this point, we might call on Dr. Sanford so that we can put the Vassar findings into the context of our discussion.

Knowledge of Students through
the Social Studies

NEVITT SANFORD

WE HAVE THOUGHT of our project as being action research, as it is sometimes called. This means that the program not only embraces services—that is, psychiatry and counseling—but also effects changes. In other words, when research results are fed back to the college community, we have thought this might conceivably induce certain changes which we would then study.

We think of ourselves as working within a social system, and we imagine that the social system changes as a foreign body, such as ourselves, is introduced into it. We know that we have changed somewhat since we have been there, and we believe that there have been certain repercussions throughout the body of the college. This is particularly important when it comes to studying students in the way that we do. It was to us rather unthinkable that we could actually interview a group of students several times a year throughout a four-year period, trying to learn about their values and attitudes, without supposing that those attitudes and values would change as a result of the students' interaction with us. So the only recourse was to make a virtue of necessity and to predict that the attitudes and values of our sample of interviewees would be different from those of the students whom we did not interview.

I want to make a remark, too, about the scolding that we do when we report psychological findings on students. It is unfortunate, but anything we say about anybody in psychological terms sounds a little bit like scolding, because of the kinds of words we use. But I think the students at Vassar have shrewdly observed that criticisms of them or criticisms of today's students are really mainly criticisms of the world in which they live, and I think, as a matter of fact, the students at Vassar have liked us better the more we have scolded them, because they have seen that the more we scold them, the more ammunition we give them for their attacks upon the world in which they live.

I believe it is fair to say that the cooperation of the students at Vassar with our research, which has always been very good, has never been better than this year, after we have made available to the students some of the research findings. Our interviewees, whom we are seeing now for the third year, have been on deck as promptly as ever, even after they have read our critique of the students; and the turnout of the seniors this spring for the senior testing was the best we have ever had.

I think this means that the students see in this work something that is interesting to them, something that concerns them, and which might supply the basis for action that they might like to take respecting the college.

It seems, as a matter of fact, that the amount of liveliness in student editorials devoted to changing this or that aspect of the college has increased this year, since our work has been available to the students. This is an interesting point suggested by Dr. Riesman. Is this wonderful cooperativeness that we have enjoyed another example of the adaptability or "acceptingness" of the students, or is it something else?

Our evidence suggests that students like to be told the truth about themselves and that they can use it. I think this is fairly fundamental; it is the need of individuals to evaluate themselves, to get evidence that what they have been thinking about themselves is on the right track and the chaos of young people, children, students—all those who have no external means for supporting their conjectures about themselves—is impossible to overestimate. So I think we are usually on the right track when we tell people the truth about themselves in circumstances which permit them to use that truth. My hope is that this is part of the reason that the students at Vassar continue to accept our program despite the hardships which it sometimes entails for them and despite the criticism which sometimes seems to be directed their way.

Studying personality development

I should like also to make a general remark about this matter of applying psychology, psychiatry, and the new social sciences in educational settings. It is quite true that we have conceived of our task as one of making psychiatry and psychology available to education, but I wish to point out that this has not meant to us that we were going to "psychiatricize" the whole thing, or bring the whole business within the psychological frame of values. We have considered that we are mainly studying personality development in general, and we are studying it in the college in much the same way we would study it at any other place. We do not consider that all of our findings will be applicable in educational settings, not now at any rate, and we would certainly hope that findings about development in general in young people could be applied in various other settings besides educational ones.

And similarly, we consider that some of the developmental goals with which we are concerned might not be favored as much by college education as by some other kind of process that could be used with young people today. In other words, we are talking here about "aims" in a very simple sense of the word, and we have thought it wise to segregate some of the kinds of aims, such as education, maturity, adaptation to social roles, and various other virtues which we at different times like to see developed in people. In our view these concepts can be defined separately. Education, health, maturity, social adaptation, and other virtues, such as social responsibility, creativity, and the like, are independently variable, and they do not necessarily intercorrelate very highly.

That is to say, we want to conceive of a person who can be highly educated, but yet quite immature and quite unhealthy, just as we would consider that a person can be quite healthy without benefit of education; and we are inclined to define education in the strict sense of the word as the inculcation of the symbols of the culture and not to confuse it with the total development of the total individual, and above all not to suppose that all of these benefits go together.

It is commonly supposed nowadays that if we can somehow have a mature person, then automatically we have a healthy and an educated person. I should say, far from it. We would be better off to consider that some of these values might have to be sacrificed to others in the end. So far are we from being able to conceive of one over-all "good" that we are actually in a position where we may have to decide sometimes whether we should prefer education or health or maturity.

Well, I say this because it is very important that we make clear to liberal educators that we are not taking the position that health in some sense of the word is the overriding value and that everything else that happens is somehow subsidiary to that end. Far from it.

In the reports we have made so far, I think what has been most interesting to people has been: (*a*) the material about the so-called peer culture or student society, such as is found in Mervin Freedman's paper,[1] (*b*) findings on differences between freshmen and seniors, and (*c*) some of our findings on the alumnae.

Peer culture among women

So much has been said about the peer society that I don't need to go into that, except to point out one or two things. One is that our results, of course, concern women, and I think that in research such as that reported by Dr. Jacob, it would be important to keep the sexes separate, that it would be quite interesting to see all of these generalizations made for men and for women separately instead of throwing the two together. That might, as a matter of fact, explain some discrepancies between what we have found at Vassar and what is regarded as quite general the country over.

One thing I want to say in addition about our observations of the peer group is that we should have a differentiated conception of this, that we should consider the possibility that different students accept the prevailing peer culture and participate in student society for different reasons. Acceptance of peer culture is a general phenomenon, but when it comes to doing something about it, we need some further analysis to tell us what the motives

[1] Freedman, "The Passage through College," in *Personality Development During College Years*, Nevitt Sanford (ed.), [entire issue] *Journal of Social Issues*, Vol. XII (1956), No. 4.

that are working in the students are. There is quite a difference between the student who participates fully in the peer culture because it is a comfortable, convenient way of meeting certain difficulties in a certain phase of one's life and the student who participates in it because he is totally lacking in any kind of inner direction and totally in need of some kind of external group to tell him what to do and what not to do.

And then there are those for whom the peer group means everything because it is a means for escaping some difficult and ambiguous relationship with the family, and there are those for whom the peer group takes over the functions of authority. Actions that we take with respect to the peer group ultimately must depend on the nature of the case. A differentiated diagnosis probably has to be made in some of these instances.

I cannot refrain from making a remark, too, on the discussion concerning changing the social climate of a college by composing the student body by means of selection. This actually is something that will have to be seriously considered, I think. Personality testing has developed to an extent that it is not inconceivable that one can identify in, say, high school seniors, some of the kinds of people one needs for making one's community a differentiated one, and in proportions that are proper.

The question was raised this afternoon, what proportion of dissident or somewhat different students do you need in order to make that group strong enough to sustain itself in a college, but not so strong that it tends to dominate the whole campus? This is a fascinating problem. I suppose it might be called human engineering, or something of the sort. It is somewhat frightening to think of setting up a human community according to some plan of that kind.

I am told that whoever finds some means for selecting students who will be successful in college will have found something that will be used by the colleges, however unhumanistic this might be. I mean, if we know that a certain kind of student with certain attitudes and a certain outlook is the kind who promises to be most successful in college, there is no way of preventing the college from trying to get that kind of student by the use of whatever tests are available. The way to do this is not by the Rorschach or the Thematic Apperception Test; you can do it much more effectively, more fairly and with much less expense, by means of objective tests. That is to say, you can identify students who, because of their similarity to students who have been successful before, can be regarded as statistically most likely to succeed. As a matter of actual fact, Vassar would like to push ahead with some work of that kind.

Let me turn now to remarks about the alumnae and some remarks about the differences between freshmen and seniors.

Findings on alumnae

Since we have devoted quite a bit of time and energy to studying alumnae I should report some of our results. Something that has not been reported elsewhere bears on the question: Are today's students really different from the students of the earlier generation?

In turning to the students we teach today, as opposed to those that we may have taught in former times, we have to guard against the frequently somewhat jaundiced outlook of the old-timer. Our nostalgia for the good old days, before the War, before the depression, or before World War I, or when we were students can easily lead us into undue viewings with alarm. What shall we call the Golden Age of the American college? If one is inclined to glorify the more distant past, he has only to read Ernest Earnest to discover that compared with some of the best colleges of the nineteenth century the average college of today is a stronghold of serious scholarship. To come to more recent times, in the good old days of Richmond College, Class of 1929, our lack of interest in national affairs was, as I recall, the despair of our history professor.

Vassar in 1929–35, to judge from the reports of a group of alumnae whom we have recently had the opportunity to study, had her fair share of "prom-trotters" and "raccoon-coat types," of girls who came to college because it was the thing to do and who had no other purpose but to have a good time, and stay in college.

Yet it does seem to be a common opinion among educators that today's students are different. This is not to deny, of course, that they still have much in common with students of former times. It seems they would have to have, if we consider that in both instances we are dealing with people in late adolescence responding to the same general types of college environment.

Actually, it is very difficult to secure reliable information on the point. Surveys of student attitudes and values hardly existed prior to 1930, and until quite recently they were very rarely carried out. The one thoroughgoing study of the thirties, T. Newcomb's study of the changing attitudes of Bennington College students, seems to bear evidence of differences then and now.

Newcomb showed that as students passed through college their attitudes changed more and more in the direction of liberalism. They came to resemble more and more closely the outlook of the majority of the faculty. These results cannot be duplicated today. With respect to political and social issues students are generally conservative when they enter college and generally conservative when they leave, and this despite the fact that faculties, by and large, have remained liberal in the sense of the New Deal.

It is not uncommon for students to say that it is a good idea to adopt a liberal façade in order to make a good impression on important faculty members. This is a curious and rather depressing state of affairs. It seems more natural, to those of our generation at any rate, for the youth to be adventurous, rebellious, full of wild ideas about changing the world, while their elders, the faculty and administration, urge restraint and common sense. Yet today we may observe a general reversal of roles, in which the faculty tries to arouse, stimulate, capture the imagination of a cautious, practical, hardheaded student body whose main idea seems to be to let well enough alone.

Another approach to the study of differences between the present generation and those of the past is to survey the attitudes and values of college graduates of various generations and to compare these with what is found in the current generation. Then, by obtaining the recollections of the graduates, examining their college records, studying the times in which they went to college, it is possible to make reasonable inferences concerning what these graduates were like when they were in college.

In our research at Vassar, we have been able to administer the same test battery to five successive classes of current freshmen and seniors and to various groups of alumnae. The test battery comprises a number of scales, about forty, for measuring various attitudes, values, modes of thought, personality dispositions, which have been judged to be significant for education. The alumnae groups that we have studied most intensively are the Class of 1904, and representatives of the Classes of 1929–1935.

The Class of 1904

The Class of 1904, as compared with the current generation of students, might be described as good old-fashioned conservatives. The emphasis is on good and old-fashioned. In other words, what we find in this group of women is genuine conservatism as contrasted with the pseudo-conservatism which is common today. In this class highly conservative attitudes in politics and economics are accompanied by a very strong accent on individual freedom and on tolerance of various kinds of minorities.

Today's students, or college-educated people under, say, thirty years of age, who are as conservative as the Class of 1904, show far less regard for individual freedom and far more regard for tolerance.

As compared with today's students, the Class of 1904 has more respect for authority, more social responsibility, greater moral strictness, greater firmness, or perhaps fixity, of opinion and attitude, more structure and organization in personality. What is particularly striking is the fact that these traits are accompanied, in these older women, by tolerance, independence of judgment, complexity of outlook, psychological-mindedness, value for the intellect and respect for the freedom of others, to a markedly greater extent than is true in the case of contemporary students.

In the typical student of today respect for authority, moral strictness and the like are very likely to be accompanied by intolerance, dependence, simplicity, and emotional and intellectual narrowness. In other words, what we seem often to encounter in today's students is a kind of premature maturity or perhaps pseudo maturity, something which very probably has to undergo considerable reorganization before it emerges as the real thing.

Another interpretation is that the outlook of 1904 students is something that they have worked out for themselves, whereas in today's students a similar outlook has the aspect of having been imposed or perhaps expropriated from outside. There is no way of knowing with certainty how much of the outlook of the 1904 students was already present when they were in college and how much of it has been determined by age and by experience after college.

I am inclined to argue that the students of 1902–1904 were different from those of today in much the way that has been described. For one thing, the outlook of the 1904 students resembles rather closely that which is usually regarded as nineteenth-century liberalism, something which certainly persisted in the early part of this century.

Again, students entering the women's colleges at the turn of the century had backgrounds that differed in certain significant ways from those of students entering college today. For example, since 1904, there has been an increasing tendency for Vassar students to be the daughters of businessmen and a decreasing tendency for them to be the daughters of educators, clergymen, or men with literary professions. Similarly, there has been a marked decrease in the frequency of cases in which the mother was a teacher, 16 percent in 1904, 2 percent in 1954. We should expect such differences in background to be associated with those differences in outlook that have been described. A difference in the times, and a corresponding difference in outlook, seems also to be reflected in the fact that 38 percent of those members of the Class of 1904 who answered our questionnaire have remained unmarried. This figure may be compared with the 10 percent which would hold today for people four or five years out of college. Of the 1904 respondents who are married, the average age at the time of marriage was twenty-nine and a half. Members of the present senior class expect to be married at twenty-three, on the average; the present freshman class, at twenty-two.

We have gathered other data on classes from the twenties and from the early forties to bolster our argument, that the attitudes found in these graduates right now actually corresponded to the times that existed in our country when they were in college having their opinions formed.

The Classes of 1929–35

Concerning the Classes of 1929–35, our information has been derived from an intensive study of fifty representatives of these classes. These women came to the campus in groups of ten, to stay for three days, while being subjected to a wide variety of psychological tests and interviews, administered by a staff of eleven. In attitudes and values, as shown by the tests, this group of subjects resembled the current students more than they resembled the Class of 1904. Little of the nineteenth-century brand of liberalism was to be found; both the liberalism and the conservatism found in this group were distinctly modern in their tone. The group as a whole was more diversified than the current student body.

Looking at the college years of this group of alumnae we find little to suggest that 1929–35 was a Golden Age of learning in the college. Undoubtedly there were as many "socially oriented" students in college primarily for a good time then as now. In listing the benefits of their college education this group of alumnae put "contact and friendship with congenial people" at the top; just as do entering freshmen today. But in our opinion there is at least one large and important difference between the student body of today and that of 1929–35; the latter was more varied, more sharply differentiated, it contained a larger proportion of quite distinctive people. The same or very similar types of students can be identified now as then, but in 1929–35, it was possible to find far more vivid representatives of these types. If a young woman was a "prom-trotter," she was likely to be so in a whole-hearted or all-out fashion—and similarly if she was a scholar or an athlete. Today the accent of student culture on moderation and leveling seems to have done its work rather well.

Students not to blame

In calling attention to these possible social and cultural determinants of some current attitudes, I do, of course, make an effort to understand some of these changes in the light of social history. One may express the hope that through increasing our understanding of the situation of today's students, we may decrease our

inclination to blame them.   For that matter, I suppose we ourselves might escape blame by attaching sufficient importance to
events and circumstances outside the college or university.   Still,
we may do well to ask ourselves what our role is in all this, and
whether an appraisal of the problem, along the lines that have
been suggested, has any implications for action on our part.

One thing seems clear, it does no good to reproach students for
their conformity, as some teachers are wont to do.   It is too easy
for students to look at their teachers and make the same accusa-
tion.   Teachers, like students, live in a social system that defines
their roles and statuses, and not many care to take the risks involved in kicking over the traces. This students see plainly. Again,
the inclination to solve ethical dilemmas by noting what the others
are going to do is by no means limited to students.

Again, my generalizations about students of today do not add
up to a statement that they are unresponsive to adult leadership.
Rather, I should be inclined to point to a default in such leadership, another sign of the times.   This is a period of general reorientation with respect to values.   For some time now parents
have been quite uncertain about what, if anything, to demand of
their children.   Similar uncertainty is reflected in the divided
councils of the college.   It has been our observation that a major
reason college freshmen gravitate so readily to the peer culture is
that real alternatives are not readily available to them.   There is
no visible adult community in which the student is encouraged
to find a place.   Yet, in my experience, whenever a plan or program or policy that is based on genuine values and shorn of all
hypocrisy and hokum, is laid before students in an understandable
way, there is rarely any failure to win their enthusiastic cooperation or allegiance.

Finally, I should be reluctant to reject the student culture out
of hand.   It is quite possible that you and I have simply outlived
our times.   This is what Dr. Kerr was saying, I think.   And we
are trying to judge what is going to be the culture of tomorrow by
the standards of yesterday.   It may turn out that the way to
manage ethnic or racial diversity is to encourage everybody to
become just alike, and that the way to decide moral questions is
by group consensus.   But I do not see how you and I, as products

of the age of individualism, can be expected to change at this late date.

Differences between seniors and freshmen

Now, I want to present something about the differences between seniors and freshmen. I think we are dealing with a problem which has an important statistical aspect; that is to say, if we talk about the whole student body at Vassar, I think we could confirm pretty much what Professor Jacob had to say.

You see, if you simply take the whole student body and speak of them as a group, you find the same kinds of things that Dr. Jacob described. But when we compare our freshmen with our seniors, differences are the order of the day, and these are really quite striking. And one could argue, I think, that this is what we should pay attention to, because if there are some students who are really changing in the desired direction, then they are the ones who should offer us clues as to how we might act so as to induce such changes in more people. And what is interesting is the fact that the desirable things encountered in our seniors go hand in hand with something which we can only call instability or mild disturbance, or something of that kind. I shall try to dramatize this by quoting from a Vassar senior:

"People talk about the problems of adolescence; if you ask me, they're nothing compared to the problems of late adolescence or young adulthood, whatever you want to call it." This senior, an honor student, had just finished recounting the major events and experiences of her college career: an intellectually exciting freshman year; growing disillusionment and dissatisfaction in the sophomore year; a soul-trying change of major at the beginning of the junior year, a decision to do what she wanted rather than to live mainly according to other people's expectations; and now, uncertainty as to whether she could maintain her change of direction, doubt that she had done the right thing. She said she felt "less sure about things than when a freshman," "confused about what has gone on," "more in a fog now than then."

This picture is not unusual. Actually, our research at Vassar College has shown that seniors, on the average, are more unstable or "upset," more uncertain about themselves and about life than are freshmen.

Is this instability of the seniors mainly a result of being in college four years and reaching the point of leaving, or is it an effect of education? If the latter, is it necessarily so? Does liberal education tend to upset people, or is it that people with greater susceptibility to being upset remain for four years of college while others drop out? Is the phenomenon that we have observed general, or is it to be found only in particular kinds of colleges or universities?

The typical freshman

The typical freshman begins her college life with eagerness and confidence. She is proud to be a member of the college community and wants to live up to the honor of having been admitted. Knowing fairly well what the next few years hold for her, she is relatively untroubled by questions of what to do or be. She is oriented primarily to the social group, and her very considerable social skill is freely displayed. She is friendly, polite, and, at least in her external aspect, poised. She participates comfortably and uncritically in the values of her family and home community, has high respect for our social institutions, and, toward the powers that be, she is deferential and uncomplaining. This last extends even to psychological testing. Freshmen approach their tests, on the first day of school, with eager compliance; the crowded auditorium in which they labor for two hours is sensationally quiet; and—oh, joy to the researcher—all the test items are completed!

In sum, the typical entering freshman is idealistic, sociable, well organized, and well behaved. Small wonder that on the standardized personality tests, she scores as a pretty sound and healthy specimen.

More than this, the evidence is that the first year of college is for the typical student a happy time. Things go according to her optimistic expectations. Her academic preparation for college, about which she may have worried, turns out to be adequate, courses prove to be interesting, some of them exciting, and social experiences are reassuring and gratifying. Her fellow students are as friendly, accepting, helpful about lining up dates, as she has dared hope.

If the first testing session is serious business, the second, on the next day, has the aspect of a festival. The freshmen now arrive in pairs or small groups, all are talking, gaily or earnestly, and it may be necessary to ask for order. By now everybody has made one or more new friends.

But this stable and happy freshman, as has been suggested, is in for some eye-opening and disillusioning, and broadening and maturing, experiences. By midway of her senior year, the chances are that she will feel rather confused, frustrated, anxious, and will look back on her freshman year as a remote and happy time. To quote our senior honor student again, "I think of my freshman year as perfectly wonderful."

The typical senior

On a variety of tests, including some that are widely used in psychiatric diagnosis, seniors score higher, that is, in regard to disturbance, than do freshmen. Seniors report more depression, more self-criticism, more anxiety and doubt, more consciousness of conflict, more hostile complaints against the environment, more unusual fantasies and behavior patterns, more disturbances in physiological functioning.

Disturbances of a truly serious and incapacitating nature are very rare; and it is possible that the picture the seniors give is due in part to their greater ability to report the difficulties that they have. But interviews with seniors leave no doubt that they have something real to report. Quotations will show something of their frame of mind.

When I came as a freshman I thought of having fun. I don't think now that life is much fun.

I can't seem to make value judgments. I'll say this works for them but not for me. I'm forever standing in the middle of the road.

Connie has been afraid she wouldn't get married. Now she's engaged and more relaxed.

When you're in college, as contrasted with school, you find you're no longer the big wheel. You find you're not so special. Anything that is done has to be done in your own small way.

I thought as a freshman I really was free and independent; now I feel immature in social relations and in values.

Recently I found myself about to get married. It was hard to get out of it for fear of hurting someone.

Freshman year was a gay, Ivy League year. By the end of the sophomore year boys in college seemed much too young. I was quite intolerant. This year I'm seeing people quite a bit older.

I still don't know what part the intellectual will play in my life.

At first I was involved with a lot of people. Now I feel inadequacy in getting to know people personally.

College has been confusing. The administration and faculty present the whole thing as intellectual. The girls don't see it that way.

I was thinking of going to such-and-such a university. But there is this whole feeling about school. I resent the authority and discipline of school.

As you will have noted, there is more in these quotations than confusion and gloom and doubt; there are also some vivid signs of growth. More precisely, there are signs of striving for valued personal objectives, for serious purpose, for independence, for realism, for self-respect, for wholeness, for intimacy. This is a crucial point. The greater instability of seniors is all of a piece with their better education and greater maturity.

Seniors are better educated in the sense of having more knowledge of their cultural heritage and of having absorbed more of the value system of the college. Seniors have more cultivated tastes, broader interests, greater attachment to the things of mind. They are less authoritarian, less conventional and conforming, less fundamentalist in religious outlook; they show more awareness and appreciation of the diversity of points of view and standards adopted by others, and are more liberal in their views on interpersonal relationships. Seniors also show in their test performances more signs of trained intellects. They are well ahead of the freshmen in flexibility of thinking, capacity to suspend judgment, tolerance of ambiguity, in skepticism, criticalness, realism.

As compared with freshmen, seniors are more "liberated." They are more assertive, rebellious, adventurous; less passive, less modest, less submissive; they have greater breadth of consciousness, more self-insight, more familiarity with their inner lives. At the same time they are more discriminating in their perceptions and less compulsive in the control of their social behavior. They show less stereotyping in their perception of the sexes and of sex roles, greater differentiation in their ideas of what they might do without endangering their conception of themselves as women. Seniors are more diversified; that is, they differ more among themselves than freshmen differ among themselves.

It is of some interest to note the responses of the seniors to our tests if we recall those of the freshmen. Upperclassmen always have to be rounded up for psychological tests, and our seniors have been no exception. Our first testing session with them, in 1953, was a college requirement. They objected; they were put off both by the requirement and by the tests themselves. They had been taught, they said, that you can't give yes-and-no answers to important questions. Since then we have sought the cooperation of the senior class as an organized group, appearing before them to explain just what we wanted to do and why, and answering all the usual lay criticisms of psychological tests. By appealing to students who missed the group testing session, we have been able to corral 90 percent of the seniors.

Reasons for instability of seniors

How may the greater instability of the seniors be explained? We may eliminate at once the possibility that the more stable students have dropped out of college before reaching the senior year; the contrary is the case; and, moreover, the differences that concern us are found when the same people are tested once as freshmen and again as seniors. The instability of seniors is the result of an interplay of factors arising from their temporary situation in life, from the society and culture outside the college, and from the senior's phase of development.

Outstanding in the senior's situation is, of course, the fact that she is about to leave college. After more than three years of increasing adjustment to academic life she must now get ready to "face the world," make crucially important decisions, lose the emotional support of her fellow students—all this while academic pressures are as great as ever. The senior has considerable ground for her fear that the society she is about to enter, or re-enter, will emphasize values that are different from her own. To be educated in a liberal college is by definition to acquire attitudes and values that differ in kind or quantity from those that prevail in our society at large. The senior is also up against the fact that in our society there is no respected and clearly defined place for the liberally educated person who is not identified with some accomplishment or activity. The emphasis is on doing, not being; and unfortunately the doing involved in being a wife and mother does not usually bring much recognition. The old problem of career versus marriage, which is as perplexing for the college woman now as it ever was, is not merely her problem; it is a sociological and ideological dilemma in which our whole society is involved.

But neither her temporary situation nor the state of the social and cultural world would be particularly upsetting for the senior had she not been growing apace, and were she not now in a particular developmental phase. She has thrown off traditional values without having fully established values of her own. She has let go the external controls she relied on as a freshman, but inner controls are still in the process of formation. She has rejected old self-identities; but her new one has not yet jelled.

Thus she may wonder whether attitudes and values now felt to be a part of herself can be sustained once she loses the support of the college community. She may feel that she has been educated for the best of all nonexistent worlds.

The question of who or what she is going to be may have been put many times before, but this time the answer has an aspect of being for keeps. She is afraid that the new identity of educated woman may not be adequate to the demands of afterlife. Since she very probably expects to marry fairly young and to become a mother, she may sense a conflict between what she has been educated for and what awaits her. Matters are not improved by the thought that having had such a good education, perhaps the best, one ought to be able to manage these dilemmas.

It is not surprising that many seniors are unable to bear the tension. Forsaking their real selves, they seek immediate relief by going all out for some clear-cut but limited identity—overdoing their identification with the values of the college, or rejecting the college completely in favor of home and home community, or announcing determinedly for a high-level career, or most commonly, rushing into marriage with the thought that this will settle everything.

Differences from college men

The situation seems to be different with young men. It is an impression, based on experience as a teacher and on verbal reports by college and university health departments, that in college men, the crisis about identity most often occurs in the sophomore year, in connection with the choice of a major with its implications for professional identity. Once this choice has been securely made, there seems to be increasing stability, and increasing integration with the larger society, through the junior and senior years.

One may ask whether the uncertainty and confusion of the senior women is a good thing. The answer is that like all developmental crises, it is potentially a very good thing indeed. Largely a result of growth, it is a necessary condition for continued growth.

Liberal education aims high. It is out to produce people who can improve society rather than merely adjust to it—women who can decide what women's roles should be rather than merely fit themselves into what exists. The liberally educated woman should have a sense of identity that does not depend, for its stability, upon her assuming and maintaining any particular social role. She should not have to define herself as a career woman or as a wife and mother, or as a widow or divorcee, in order to have a comfortable sense of who she is.

The uncertain senior is headed in this general direction. She is still striving to broaden and deepen her personality. She is on the road to becoming a richer and more complex person. She is more unstable than the typical freshman because she has more to stabilize, less certain of who she is because more possibilities have entered the picture. She is striving for integration on a higher level, and the approach of graduation catches her before this process has gone far enough. Unstabilized as she is, she must either continue to grow or else go backward. Her fate depends heavily upon the kind of situation she now enters.

Alumnae reachieve stability

Whether or not a woman, in our group of alumnae from twenty to twenty-five years after college, had gone on in the direction in which she was headed at the time of graduation, seemed to depend a great deal on the man she married, on whether or not he provided support for her college-bred values. In general, the value outlook of alumnae resembles that of freshmen somewhat more closely than it resembles that of seniors. Undoubtedly this reflects in considerable part the stabilization achieved by alumnae as they moved into responsible social roles; but very likely it also reflects a certain retreat, under the impact of Main Street, from the ideals and aspirations that excited them as seniors. In some alumnae, certainly, a more or less suitable self-conception had been achieved by the forcible exclusion of some preferences and inclinations. But these excluded patterns were still very much alive, sometimes prompting implicit assumptions that they would some day be attended to, sometimes giving rise to guilt and regret, or even to a nagging sense of self-betrayal.

Many of the alumnae took the occasion of their visit to Vassar for the assessment project to do some serious stock-taking of themselves. Some were stimulated to make new departures, or rather, actually to begin projects or activities that had been vaguely contemplated in the past; for example, one of our subjects immediately embarked on a long-postponed writing project, another registered for graduate work in education, another went into psychotherapy.

According to theory, the conditions that make for growth and those that make for instability are basically the same; essential to both is stress of sufficient intensity to require adjustive changes. The development of the senior to her present status is a result of stresses in the past; and her present unstable condition is best described as a state of heightened educability.

If we were interested in stability (health) alone, we would do well to have a program designed to keep freshmen as they are. Or, we might decide in advance what a suitable role for women should be and proceed to educate them for precisely that. But the college that would promote individuality and wholeness must stir up its students; it must create necessities for personal restructuring. It must also, of course, try to keep the stress within reasonable limits, and to arrange things so that the adjustive changes are educationally desirable.

Our evidence is that Vassar does stir its students up, quite a number of them at any rate. The question is: Will the desired changes stick? Or, more important, what might make them stick? Since we cannot count on the major society to contribute to this end, we have to think further about what the college might do. The facts and arguments presented here suggest two lines of experimentation. The one would be directed to some kind of prolongation of the educational process. It would seek to capitalize on the senior's instability and openness to new experience, in promoting still further growth and in shoring up the new self-structure she attains. We might think in terms of a kind of staged withdrawal from the college environment, for an example, a year of graduate study at the same institution or a work-study program for the last year or two of college.

The other suggestion would be that we explore means to induce earlier in the college course the state of educability found in seniors. It is conceivable that some of the benefits of leaving and of being forced to make important choices, could be attained by arranging for a sharp change, after two years, from one kind of educational program to another, perhaps from a highly structured program to a slightly unstructured one.

Toward the definition of goals

The liberal colleges, in trying to promote the development of the individual as a whole, have had to do without agreed definitions of particular developmental goals. There are few clearly stated hypotheses, and fewer established facts, concerning relations between educational procedures and educational outcomes. The colleges proceed according to tradition and practical wisdom. Perhaps they have not done too badly. But it may be asked whether it is not time that the resources of social science were brought to bear upon this whole problem. From the point of view of the social scientist, higher education is a vast and relatively untouched field. At Vassar, we have merely begun to explore it.

In conclusion, I think the major problem for future investigation is how to account for the changes that do occur in college. At this stage of our knowledge, we will do best to make intensive studies of individuals with the use of theory and hypothesis. This will lead pretty soon to the study of the possibility of typology, that is, some sort of grouping of kinds of students, and predictions as to what kinds of students change under what kinds of conditions.

I think the kind of research that Dr. Riesman was calling for, comparisons among colleges with the use of the same instruments, will happen anyway; it is quite to be expected; since our tests have been available, and they have all been published now, we have actually sent them to thirty different colleges who wanted to begin using them immediately.

I think it is quite in the cards that the colleges are going to be using such instruments in assisting themselves. I would make a final plea for the college research department as one means for getting the necessary research done. This should go on even while some large, over-all agency is performing the desired "market research" on all the colleges. I think the particular college will do better, and it will keep this kind of research humanistic, if it has its own research department and if the situation is one in which the researchers have to live with the people on whom they are doing the research.

Discussion

Miss Goddard: I should like to make three comments that relate to some extent to what Dr. Sanford was saying and go back to one of the points that Dr. Riesman made. They all relate to the question you ask of what the major questions of educational policy which confront educators are.

I think the question that is important to the freshmen as they come, to the seniors as they leave, is the campus climate of the freshman year. Dr. Riesman made the point that students come to college expecting a great deal and then find there less than they expected. I would say that a great many students do not find the academic challenge they thought they were going to get. They do not find, I think, so strong a group opinion among the faculty as they expected. If there were more real demands, real challenges, real discussions of ideas, I think there would be fewer façades of liberalism, which Dr. Sanford pointed out as one of the things you find in college; I think, too, there wouldn't be so much emphasis on the student culture simply because there would be strong motivations, any one of which the student could follow.

The second point I would make is that I feel that there is an unfortunate hiatus between the academic process and many other spheres of student life, and it seems to me that if there is validity in students doing things in addition to studying history, for instance, then the relationship between these two forces must be made increasingly clear.

And the third point that I should like to make refers to the whole question of the insecure seniors. I think it would be very good if it were possible for students to make more real decisions while they are going through the four years of being an undergraduate. At the same time, I myself am an advocate of trying to preserve a certain amount of the ivory tower in college. I think it is unfortunate that we are always saying that we must have college as a preparation for "living." Can we resolve the matter of making choices and still permit the preservation of an ivory tower?

MR. RIESMAN: Does the curriculum seem to be so much a fact of the natural state of things, like the bomb, that it seems hopeless to a student to do anything about it?

MISS GODDARD: Yes. What I was about to say is that I think certain things about it seem hopeless enough or so big that students turn to peripheral things.

MR. BAKKEN: I think the point regarding experience-centered learning, as Dr. Jacob called it, complements what Miss Goddard said; namely, that the way a student finds challenge is not in these peripheral things. It is in experience-centered learning which has the curriculum as its focus.

In response to Dr. Riesman's point, I think it is true that the student finds a certain impossibility in the curriculum that forces him outside it. And I would hope that some technique could be found that would enable him to work in the things directly affecting him at that time, which are largely curricular. I do not think this opportunity has been developed in most of our colleges.

The value of instability

CHAIRMAN KILLIAN: Professor Sanford, you spoke in terms of approbation of this sense of instability, uncertainty, and disturbance that you see in students in women's colleges. You indicated that this did not exist in the student bodies of men's colleges, because men begin early to find a professional objective; they select their major and move on, and they have a sense of allegiance to a professional career or field of endeavor they set out to pursue. Do you feel this is a weakness in the education of men, that they do not have this instability that occurs as a result of the humanistic curriculum in the women's colleges?

MR. SANFORD: Yes, I do, and I think that it is in the nature of things. It is one reason for having women's colleges, by the way. Actually I would regard the increasingly professional orientation of men's colleges as a threat to the traditional values of liberal education and as a sign of the times; when the men's colleges perforce yield to such threats, it is very comforting to think that the women's colleges don't have to. The point I am emphasizing is that I do think there is an important sex difference here, and in our surveys of the values and attitudes of students, this ought to be taken into account.

MR. GIDEONSE: Is there any evidence from good coeducational colleges with regard to a difference between the men and the women in the sophomore and the senior years?

MR. SANFORD: I don't have any. My remark was based on experience rather than on objective data. Most of it comes from the University of California where, at the counseling center and at the student psychiatric service, a common type of problem is the matter of the false vocational choice. For instance, there is the student who is in the junior year and discovers he really doesn't want to be a doctor, at all, and for him this goes to the very center of his being. I think many women have a problem of just as great intensity, but it is postponed until the senior year.

NATHAN M. PUSEY: I want to ask a question. As you described this heightened educability of the senior woman at Vassar, you seemed to imply that that somehow suggested that the educational experience has been a successful one. Yet, as I listened to you, it seemed to me that a sufficient explanation for this was in the mere fact that she was leaving one society and had to find a place in a new one.

MR. SANFORD: The two are certainly aspects of the same general phenomenon. One could check on it, of course, by seeing if a similar state of upset is to be encountered among high school seniors who are also in a leaving type of situation.

MR. PUSEY: That wouldn't be an exact parallel, going from high school to college.

MR. SANFORD: No. They have some direction already laid out for them. It is noticeable, of course, that some seniors do not experience this at all, even though they are about to leave. Whether or not they experience it depends on whether they have some kind of plan which is really fundamentally congenial. As we have remarked, where students are definitely committed to graduate school, they avoid being upset altogether, as do girls who have already made their decision for marriage and now foresee that they will go right into marriage. The difficulty is for those who are still unsettled with respect to these fundamental questions.

CHAIRMAN KILLIAN: But do you feel this is a reduction in educability?

MR. SANFORD: I think this is an increase in educability. I think the awareness of their own problems in the world constitutes an openness to learning on all fronts. It is really quite striking how many seniors talk sense about themselves and the world in a way that they haven't been heard to talk at all before.

As Mr. Bakken tells us, this is where they really live, and finally, they have been hit where they live, so that now they are prepared to consider fundamental philosophical questions and questions about society and life in a way that they were not doing before.

The incidence of instability

MR. JACOB: I wonder if you could give us some idea of the proportion of seniors who have this sense of uncertainty, instability, and unhappiness which contributes to their better future education.

MR. SANFORD: I told you that I was going to try to dramatize it in order to make the point. It really isn't anything very grim, you know, for most students. I cannot quite say in what proportion because I am speaking in statistical terms about the relative disturbance of the seniors as compared with freshmen. I am talking about average differences, and it is not a categorical thing. You don't say that some seniors belong to the upset group and others do not. It is a matter of degree, and I am taking the experience from interviewing seniors and using that to bolster and to interpret the statistical findings, so that I really couldn't name any proportion of seniors who are in the upset group as compared with those who are not.

MR. JACOB: I am wondering whether in your studies it was apparent, let's say, that more girls than not had had this experience happen to them.

MR. SANFORD: I would be justified in saying what I said in the way I said it if this happened to one in five. This would be enough to make a striking statistical difference between seniors and freshmen. Actually, I suppose the average teacher feels quite happy if he has really reached one in five of his students, and anything that would be true of one in five would be very important, I think. Of course, it won't be overwhelming because at the same time I am saying this about differences between freshmen and seniors, I am also saying that, in general, you are right in giving a picture which indicates that not a lot happens to the great rank and file of the students, and we are speaking in statistical terms in both cases. And we are both right in saying that not enough happens to the average student. I think we can all agree to that, but we can also say that something does happen to a quite sizable proportion of them, and we should find out what makes this happen and see if this doesn't give us some hints about how it could happen to more people.

Elmer Ellis: Do your data show how many of these senior girls are engaged? Does that make a difference?

Mr. Sanford: I don't believe so. That would make a difference.

Mr. Ellis: I am sure it would make a difference in our co-educational schools, too.

Mr. Pusey: One of the things that hasn't been mentioned in this discussion is, I believe, relevant. It seems to me a very large number of the people coming to Harvard College now begin to work for admission to graduate school almost before they are admitted. In a sense, this does appear at first blush to have been working against liberal education. The motivation of trying to get into graduate school is the thing that is shaping the behavior of our undergraduates today as much as anything in our experience. Three-quarters of them have that goal in mind. The students are professional-minded, but certainly this keeps them from drifting away from the academic program, or from whatever the values of the faculty are. I think that students give themselves to that willingly and with a good deal of zeal. The problem for the college therefore is to make sure that that academic experience does not let them down. It has to be a very rich thing and really first-rate. There can be no boredom in the classroom.

Uses of personality tests

Chairman Killian: Do you feel that the design of the student body through personality testing and selection is really a tenable thing, that we can have the wisdom or that we should have the authoritarianism, if you will, to try to pattern a student body, so we can get the different elements properly balanced?

Mr. Sanford: I would really be quite anxious if I were to take part in some such program as that. Testing has to be combined with counseling if it is to be right.

Let's say that if personality tests are going to be used for decisions affecting students, then the students should participate in those decisions. If we are to avoid something which really is authoritarian, then we can't use special kinds of knowledge about people, which they don't have, to make decisions affecting them which they do not fully participate in themselves. I would strongly object to the use of the personality tests for any decisions affecting students except insofar as the students participated in those decisions themselves. That means counseling. I would grant, however, that it is not inconceivable that, if we tested high school classes with such instruments as we have and scored everything and got a fair picture of how the students stood, it would not be inconceivable that we could then interview some of those students with a view to discussing with them whether or not a given college might be suitable for them, and if we really needed them to lend spice to our student body, we might be justified in recruiting them as students.

MR. GIDEONSE: I am quite in agreement with you on the authoritarian character of that kind of use of data if you don't tell the people involved; but it seems to me, if you assume that you can achieve this purpose and you also assume that you are going to achieve it by telling people the real meaning of this test to you as an institution and to them as individuals, you are making fanciful decisions as to the effect of your counseling. It means concretely that this personality test tells you that this is just the kind of rebel you need in small doses to do the right thing to your run-of-the-mine conformists, and you are going to tell him, with all the implications, about the run-of-the-mine conformists and the possibility to run elsewhere.

There is no counselor that eloquent or effective that I know of, and that is merely one example. When you think of the variety of people you would want to fit into a pattern, when you once begin to build a Utopian ivory tower and sit down and make the sample, that in itself is playing God. That is what worries me about the whole drift of this thinking.

CHAIRMAN KILLIAN: To what extent does all this emphasis on testing create a feeling of self-examination or of self-consciousness by students, so that we get, not an exuberant interest in learning, but a preoccupation with one's own introverted problems and difficulties? Are we running the hazard of creating an institutional climate and environment in which we have a preoccupation, not with the joy of learning, but rather with all the introverted, self-conscious aspects of one's own personality problems?

MR. SANFORD: Students, I think, take personality tests pretty much in their stride as long as they know they are not going to be used as a basis for any valuation that matters. We have always assured the students at Vassar that this is research, that it has nothing to do with determining their fate in any way. And that is absolutely essential.

The only way a college could really use this kind of information would be in a general way to know something about itself, with a view to constructive changes in itself. Such tests cannot, I think, be used to evaluate colleges or students, unless the person who is being evaluated is in a position to do something right now about whatever deficiencies seem to be suggested by the tests.

Values of personality tests

MR. RIESMAN: One of the things I had in mind in discussions with Frank Bowles was a problem he himself raised of students who are not, for many reasons, caught by the present run of tests, whose gifts, developments, and attitudes toward tests are more complex, and who now tend to get lost because we tend, in avoiding and minimizing personality inquiry, to rely instead on grade averages. It is the safest bet. And we may be missing people who are more creative and useful, more imaginative than the average, and who might be saved with more imaginative and evocative tests.

MR. JACOB: I wonder, too, if an adequately developed personality assessment of students is valuable in guiding the instructional process in college.

I am impressed by the way in which some of this testing has been used to section students. I do not know whether these tests are yet adequate for this purpose or if they could be made so, but it seems to me it would be a tremendously important thing to have a student take his freshman course in history or political science in a group and with an instructor with whom he might get along better and become more educable, than simply to have him dumped into the hopper of a registrar's automatic selection system and told, "You go to Section 22." Maybe we could, by the use of our instruments, at least turn the sectioning into a useful educational procedure rather than a purely administrative device.

MR. GIDEONSE: That, too, has a totalitarian implication of a sort that makes me think that Dr. Kerr's observations are understatements. In the first place, you have the unresolved question touched on a moment ago of whether you get maximum returns from putting all of category C in one class and all of B in another or from mixing them in some way determined by research.

If you begin to think that way, there is a discernible and even measurable difference between students of category C and teachers of category A, and this means that you have to classify your teachers before you assign students to them in sections, using some kind of personality testing apparatus, which implies power on the part of the department chairmen, deans, and presidents that would make them want to abdicate right away.

MR. KERR: This talk worries me a little. I wonder if it wouldn't be more democratic really to test people on their performance and evaluate them on their performance as they go along from one stage to another, rather than trying to anticipate all these things.

MR. SANFORD: I think this question is not merely a question of whether or not you make use of tests, because these kinds of decisions affecting students are frequently made on the basis of interviews—or somebody's intuition. Tests never really tell you anything that you couldn't find out by means of interviews if you took the time. The tests simply telescope the process of finding out. As for using them to predict future performance, Dr. Kerr's point is well taken. If you use this as a basis for rejecting the students, that is very poor policy indeed. If you use it as a basis of understanding students, so that you can make wiser decisions affecting them, that is an entirely different matter. I don't believe psychological testers are any more given to the misuse of information about people than other responsible specialists.

MR. PUSEY: The part of the report on Vassar that meant the most to me was the attempt to recognize the personality types of students in the student body. We talk about students as though they were one, and we all know they are not.

It would be helpful if the social scientists could identify a few categories or types of people which had some validity and which we could use as we think about structuring the curriculum and the selection of students. We should have similar categories and types in the faculty. If we could put these things together, we could talk more sensibly.

MR. SANFORD: This is the direction in which we should go, but our knowledge is pretty limited so far. It seems to me to be a matter for research at this stage rather than a matter for action. I can only agree with Professor Jacob about the experiment of George Stern in which he showed that when students are selected on the basis of significant personality types, different methods of teaching were effective, and that experiment, I think, is quite valid. But I am made anxious by the notion of sorting students out according to patterns of personality without their full participation in it.

Knowledge of this kind, however, might be helpful to the whole college, to the teachers. It would be helpful to know, for instance, the difference between an adult-oriented student and a peer-oriented student. The developmental problem for the one is different from that for the other. Do we think of a different curriculum for this difference in orientation? Or can we make the faculty aware of this kind of difference and help them to recognize that the student who is already adult-oriented presents a different problem from the student who is afraid of adults and who is trying to avoid them?

I find it very difficult to talk about this because the personality types are significant for the total development of the student, and we don't go very far in speaking about this before we get into something akin to counseling. I am inclined to think that at this stage of the game all we can do is to try to identify the types and potentialities and to make this knowledge available. People whose responsibility it is to work with students will find ways to take advantage of the knowledge and they will find ways which we at the moment cannot imagine.

The role of the faculty

CHAIRMAN KILLIAN: Is this the kind of knowledge that can be handled by faculty members rather than by psychologists or psychiatrists, or people who are expert in these fields, without making serious misinterpretations?

Mr. Sanford: The experience at Vassar has been that the effort on the part of psychiatrists and psychologists to tell faculty about students, using the terms of psychology and psychiatry, has not been very successful. The faculty does not want to be told its business by the so-called experts. We have avoided altogether talking about individual students with faculty because we do not believe that we can be of most help to faculty by participating with them in a kind of counseling activity about individual students. We see our task rather as one of discovering facts about students in general and about what goes on in college and to make this available to faculty in the hope that this will somehow, in time, change their general orientation toward students. I don't think we want to ask the faculty to become psychiatrists or counselors or psychologists. I think the teacher who counsels the student should first be a teacher who has inspired the student intellectually; the student chooses this teacher because he means something special to the student. He is a model and an inspiration rather than an expert who is going to look into the motives and the particular situation of the student.

It is worth pointing out, however, that we really don't have any literature that can be used in talking to the faculty about students. The psychiatric literature won't do; really, the resistance to that by the faculty is quite appropriate, because it is not rooted in a conception of development in normal young people, and you cannot find very much about the development of students as personalities that can be used in talking with the faculty about them.

How to get this literature? I don't see how you can get it except by research of some kind; I think this would be the approach to what, it seems to me, is the major problem on campuses, and that is that the faculties are not sufficiently interested in students. The reason they are not interested is that they don't know enough about students.

If that sounds paradoxical, I am nonetheless quite sure that it is true. They don't see students in a framework of a developmental psychology which would make each student fascinating to observe, with attention to where he is in respect to certain kinds of developmental goals.

Actually, as we know something about students, there is nothing more fascinating to observe than the struggles that develop, the regressions that occur, and so on.

If we could show the faculty that this is really the most fascinating business in the world, watching and participating in the development of young people, we would really have done something, I think.

CHAIRMAN KILLIAN: Here I think I have to say that our universities, as they have enormously expanded their research efforts, have probably at the same time greatly diminished their effectiveness in undergraduate education. This is a major problem in American education today. The attitude of the faculty toward teaching is a major problem.

This doesn't mean that the institutions are still not first-rate institutions and first-rate environments for the students who want excellence, but I do think that this kind of appraisal of the total educational opportunity is an important one both for the institution and for the student.

MR. SANFORD: I think that the main thing is to have faculty members who have time to be human beings and to enter into adult relationships with students and that there will always be a place for the kind of faculty-student relationship based on what I described as the inspiration or the model that the faculty has to offer.

MR. RIESMAN: I am sure that it is implicit in what you said that the typical psychologist and the typical psychiatrist are not the model you want for this, either. You are looking for the kind of teacher who now so rarely exists, who has the humane qualities that few psychiatrists do have and which, likewise, one might say, few teachers have.

MR. SANFORD: I think teachers as individuals have been properly resistant to attempts to make them more psychiatric, attempts to get them to enter a different profession, you might almost say. I don't believe the teacher needs to have any special expert psychological or psychiatric knowledge to do the most valuable counseling that is done by anybody.

MR. JACOB: Several questions have arisen in my mind as a result of the comments that have been made here.

Challenging the students

I thoroughly agree that we should try to capture a student's enthusiasm as soon as he comes to college. But I wonder whether an intellectual challenge is sufficient to prime the enthusiasm of the mass of students. I confess, that as I confront a fair number of the entering freshman class each year at my institution, I sense a heavy intellectual lethargy which may be a carry-over from the high school period. To try to overcome this, ought we not to concentrate the limited counseling resources and efforts we have in the freshman year or during the first two years of college? If something quite crucial does not happen to the student as he enters into the college experience, it may well cost him and the institution the chance to develop a creative relationship at any point in the college career. We obviously do not have the right number of skilled counselors to spread throughout the student body. We don't have an adequate number of skilled teachers to bring an intellectual challenge to everyone. We don't have the right number of persons who can translate intellectual stimulus into the personal experience of students and thus affect them in any fundamental way. Therefore we should consider a deliberate reorientation or reallocation of our resources, bringing to bear what we have, limited though it is, upon the most crucial period of a student's college life.

For instance, I wonder whether institutions should not concentrate great efforts on bringing to each freshman in his first few months an opportunity to know at least one faculty member who really strikes fire with him. A lasting and profound counseling relationship or personal relationship between the two might then grow.

In addition, the student might undergo in his first six months at least one experience of a nonintellectual character—though tied in with his academic program—which would shake him and make him realize very clearly that "this is not high school."

Considering the needs of the mass of students, and the tendency toward standardization in high schools, an educational strategy which attacks the problem of challenging the entering freshman is of major importance.

CHAIRMAN KILLIAN: I share this feeling very strongly. We had quite an extraordinary experience in our institution this spring when we had a visiting professor who is not an educator, but who has been closely associated with Harvard and M.I.T., and who is a very imaginative man. After a long series of consultations with students and faculty, he summed up his experience in a lecture which was both stimulating and disturbing. He took the point of view that American colleges and universities now find coming to them a group of young people who have initially an image of greatness and excellence; usually by the end of the first term or first year that image has been destroyed or in some way watered down, and so they have lost the sense of having a creative opportunity themselves to do something in college. The routine, the regimentation, the lack of contact, the lack of association with stimulating people, the lack of a technique that draws out students to do something creative and original on their own —these have stifled the sense of greatness and excellence with which they came.

His contention was that, in the kinds of institutions that he was talking about, we get students who do have a creative instinct and we do nothing to take advantage of it in the freshman year. This is the crucial point. They are therefore dropping back into routine and by the time they become sophomores or juniors they are, except for the top few, cynical.

MR. KERR: Isn't there another group which may be larger, across the country as a whole? That is the group that doesn't want to be challenged and doesn't want to participate.

I am not saying we don't have a lot of students who do want to be challenged. But I wonder if you wouldn't find in the American student body in colleges and universities a substantial proportion of students who simply don't want to be challenged, they simply don't want to be faced with decisions, they want rather to go to large classes and get lost. The problem of what you do with them is tougher than the question of what do you do with the ones who want to be challenged. They will find a way to be challenged. The tougher problem is with those who will do almost anything to avoid being challenged.

FRANK C. ABBOTT: Or who do not know whether they want to be challenged. There is an implication in what you say that they have made up their minds. The real problem is that they don't have the tools to decide whether they want to or not.

MR. SANFORD: May I continue for a moment the discussion about challenging students and about counseling. Our chief recommendation on the basis of our experience at Vassar concerns trying to set up an intellectual community in the college. Or one might put it this way. If one should ask what the size of an educational organization should be, one's answer would be that it should be small enough so that everyone in it knows everybody else rather well, that all the faculty members know all the students and all the students know all the faculty members. Our thinking has been mainly in the direction of a college within the college, or outside the college, of about one hundred students and about a dozen members of the faculty, which could be duplicated indefinitely. But as long as you have a community that is a community in the sense that everybody can interact with everybody else, it doesn't make any difference how many such communities you have.

I don't believe this can be done without a radical change in our notions about curriculum. I could not agree more, with Miss Goddard and the others, that the freshmen who arrive at Vassar are quite ready for something. They have high ideals, high expectations, and they want to be challenged. They want something to happen to them. It doesn't take very long as a result of their dealings with the college bureaucracy, of being divided among all the departments, of being pulled hither and yon by requirements of one sort or another, and of their contacts with the other students, to learn the ropes in manipulating the situation, so that the enthusiasm with which they began is dissipated.

I don't see how you can get hold of those freshmen unless you do so through a group of people who are interested in them as freshmen and prepared to go to work to educate them. I don't believe that you can do it when people represent twelve different departments and if their primary loyalty is to their own department and to getting more students into it. I believe we need some kind of integrated curriculum of general education in which these dozen faculty members participate as a unit, and which will be the same for all students, at least for the first two years.

I can support that, not by saying that integrated curricula are good or that general education is good, but simply on the ground that education has to occur in a certain kind of community, and the best way to create this community is by teaching the same students the same things at least for a period that gets them going, that gives them some conception of what it means to pursue intellectual objectives together with people who have pursued those objectives and know what they mean.

This is one direction in which I think the experience at Vassar has been leading. One proposal is to take one of the existing dormitories and make a college of it and to strive to make it more or less self-sufficient as a community, aware of its differences from the rest of the college, a student-faculty community in which "we" means "we faculty and students" rather than we students as opposed to "that other group." Another proposal is to set up a college as an independent unit outside Vassar on the farm and regard it as an experiment; and by experiment I mean a set-up in which one actually observes the effects as compared with other kinds of programs.

The need for vicarious experience

MR. RIESMAN: We want more human and humane understanding on the part of faculties; but, on the other hand, I am sure we also want more vicariousness and less experience in the college curriculum. One of the problems with Vassar is that it is in a small town. There isn't enough range of vicarious experience available in theater, in music, in personalities. And the place has to feed, therefore, too much on itself. Students believe that they can only learn in small groups. This is ridiculous. This is an ethos which they have been encouraged to believe by all sorts of pedagogical conventions about small groups and present American ideology about small groups and "shared experience." They certainly learn in large groups from the movies. They can learn even from lectures; at least students ought to learn more about how to learn from a lecture than they now do.

The satellite institution needs to have a vicarious environment available which is of some magnitude and scope and variety. It does not need to have, you might say, a built-in permanent family-like intimacy. It needs occasional intimacy or periodic intimacy; and students, in order to profit from a variety of nonintellectual, vicarious experiences, need to learn that they can do so when all tendencies in our culture seem to persuade them that they cannot.

Mr. SANFORD: That is very interesting. You and I both want the best of both worlds for these students. It seems to me the only way we can have it would be to embrace the idea of moving from one place to another. I am rather convinced on the basis of investigation of such students as we get at Vassar that at that stage they need the experience of a rather tightly organized intellectual community for a time, for two years. It gives them a taste of what this really means. I think they are just at the stage where this would be valuable. Then I should like to see them transferred to a radically different community, like the University of California, where they can have all the benefits of vicariousness that you mentioned and where the requirement of adapting themselves to a radically different environment would itself be highly stimulating and educational.

Possible advantages of satellite institutions

CHAIRMAN KILLIAN: Is there a possibility that we may be moving in the direction of a lower-division system of education, call it a junior college or what you will, in which this more intimate general educational environment will be pursued? And then the student transfers out of that into the university environment, with the upper two years of the conventional undergraduate program merging more and more with the graduate years? I wonder if this may not be a pattern that may be wise if not inevitable.

Mr. SANFORD: We are making an assumption about the stage of the development the student has reached. We are assuming the same stage of development for all, which is not the case. One seventeen-year-old may be ready for this diversified university setting right now and others won't be ready until they have had four years of college.

MR. KNIGHT: I don't think you have to move geographically to achieve the things we have been talking about.

CHAIRMAN KILLIAN: But the concept of the satellite institution within the senior institution might revolve around the introductory phase, the first two years, with a sharp break at the end of that time into the more professional, independent kind of environment.

MR. GIDEONSE: I should like to put in an earthy word of warning on this objective of establishing some type of satellite institution. Unless you make very clear the specific qualitative objectives that you have in mind, you might be encouraging one of the worst features of large educational operations, and that is the temptation of running a lot of satellite institutions with freshman and sophomore courses to produce revenue for the rest of the institution.

CHAIRMAN KILLIAN: This is the introduction of another motive.

MR. GIDEONSE: Let's not have the endorsement, for qualitative reasons, of something that is one of the worst features of educational processes and operations, as I observe them in my own area.

Possible releases from captivity

MR. RIESMAN: Our society is creating a series of periods of captivity for people. They are captives as high school students, if they don't go away. Indeed, I should like to see public boarding schools in this country with lots of scholarship aid for those whose development makes this right for them. Often students are lost for even the possibility of stimulation in college by their high school experience, as we all know.

Then they are later captives when they enter a major or a professional school and realize at thirty-five or forty years they are in the wrong slot, and unless they have private resources, they cannot possibly begin again. We tend to push these points of final decision back further and further, as our professional life takes on more and more the glamorous aspects of our society, so that people are captives of professions and life careers and goals about which they know less and less when they make the decision to enter them.

We might try to make people feel freer to move at all levels; to change their careers at any point, in other words, seems to me to provide one of the most important resources our society can use to deploy its tremendous surplus, once we stop building armaments and superhighways exclusively.

We will need many, many people in service industries to employ our population in the future, the very developments Dr. Kerr has talked about. And in long-range planning, it seems to me, one wants to think about providing subventions from loans, preferably, or from other sources, so that at each point people have alternatives and know they exist. They should know they exist through consumer research, that they have the alternatives, even if, for psychological reasons or family pressures or what not, there would be reasons for them to prefer not to have a choice.

Thus, if they are in Vassar for two years and want to go to Minnesota and it costs more, or vice versa, this can be done without their feeling they are wrong to have "invested" that much.

MR. HOWES: Mobility through easy transferability from one institution to another, so that the student can get the right thing for him at the right time instead of being regimented somehow or stuck in a strait jacket that he cannot get out of.

Development of perspective

MR. RIESMAN: If you say to some of these youngsters, don't go to college right away, take a year out—if you are a boy, maybe take your Army service now, or if you are a girl, take a job or study singing, or do any other of a number of things, such as go abroad—you find the fear, objection, anticipation of the future that we have been talking about, which gets in the way. And this is quite apart from their feeling of "I am stupid if I drop back," or "This peer group is all I know and I have to stick with them," to the next step, the feeling of wanting to marry, which comes so early among boys as well as girls and of wanting to be through early, as if life is lived on a flat plane of immediacy.

One of the things that is missing among young people today is any real perspective of this whole developmental prospect of their long future. That is one of the reasons for the drive for experiential rather than vicarious college experience; they feel as if they are going to die the day they graduate, not because of the bomb—they don't, it seems, think much about that—and not with the rationalizations we would find for the same attitude, but because, for a whole variety of reasons I don't pretend to understand, they live in the present and discount the future. The notion that they will live to be ninety is inconceivable to them. It is terribly hard to make them see that they can afford certain moratoria, indeed that these moratoria are important to them.

I ask what can be done to change that, how one can even begin to go about it, to break the chronological step and to have them feel they really have lots of time? I don't know.

MR. BAKKEN: Let me ask you, were you different in your generation? Did you have more of a perspective in this way?

MR. RIESMAN: For bad reasons, I would say; possibly for some good reasons. The girls who used to go to college spent a year coming out before they went to Vassar. The boys used to have to do more in the way of earning money in between. They taught school, which was a great help to our schools. This kind of pattern did not come from any great perspective on the future. In the depression years, of course, people postponed their graduation as much as possible in much the same way, and for much the same reason that in a period of prosperity they anticipate their graduation.

I think the point is not really that this present generation is in any respect any less mature than that generation. This anticipation is a type of greater maturity and greater adult orientation and lesser desire to be treated as children than in the more frivolous era.

Summary of the papers

CHAIRMAN KILLIAN: Perhaps a short summary is in order here, so I shall take a desperate chance at trying to hit some of the points that have been made during the discussion, at least to recall to us the specific recommendations that our three speakers made during the course of their discussion.

Dr. Riesman, I think, made four basic recommendations in his conclusion. The first was that we should have better consumer research or better methods of checking on the performance of colleges.

The second was his proposal for more satellite institutions, both as a part of the complex of larger or separate institutions or satellites within colleges, so that we could get greater variety in approach, in climate, and in method.

The third was that we ought to devise better means than those we have now for avoiding the male-vanity culture that dominates so many of our institutions.

And finally, he suggested that we should make a sharper break between college and high school than we are generally doing at the present time.

These, Dr. Riesman, were your basic recommendations other than those that were implicit in your discussion. Or would you like to add to that statement?

MR. RIESMAN: No; that is fine.

CHAIRMAN KILLIAN: In his presentation, Dr. Jacob urged that there should be a more extensive study of changing values among college students, that the material so far available is relatively small, and he would like to see a great deal more.

Next, he raised the question of whether we might not look hard at the problem of revising the conception of the mission of liberal education, of whether the present concept that liberal education is good for all students is necessarily a valid one or whether it should be limited to those who have the capacity to respond to it.

Next, he proposed that there should be more variety in liberal education, that we have too much of a pattern or single concept of what the process seeks to do, and that this variety presumably should be more in accord with the great variety of students who seek liberal education. I take it this is not unrelated to the proposal that we should have satellite institutions where different approaches are taken.

His fourth suggestion, as I noted it, was that we should seek to move from an intellectually centered curriculum to an experientially centered curriculum in our liberal arts colleges, in which there would be more opportunity to try new things and more opportunity to deal with the emotional personality factors as well as the intellectual factors that are involved in the student process. We should do more in the way of letting students make decisions by which they prosper or suffer the consequences. There is too much prescription, too much that is cut and dried, too little opportunity for the student to make mistakes and to take the consequences for making them. We all try to keep students from making mistakes so they don't suffer the consequences.

Next, he proposed that we should seek those elements of discord in the student and perhaps to exploit them to the advantage of education. Is this the proper interpretation of what you said?

MR. JACOB: Quite so.

CHAIRMAN KILLIAN: And his final point, as I recall, was a belief that the colleges should take more responsibility for the cocurriculum; that is, they should feel more of a sense of responsibility toward all of the extracurricular affairs of college students, not that they should dominate them or attempt to run them, but rather to try to set the stage for them to be more effective. Finally, he added a footnote to this, that he felt there was a great opportunity for college administrations to take direct and decisive action to get rid of outmoded organizations and cocurricular institutions that are no longer performing a useful function.

MR. JACOB: I also strongly second Dr. Riesman's conviction that we should go forward with a more intensive and significant guidance program. I think that the discovery of the personal resources of the individual student and linking these with the proper kind of educational experience is an important line of development.

CHAIRMAN KILLIAN: Right. Professor Sanford proposed that we should seek in various ways to extend the educational experience in order to continue the effect of instability and the consequent educability that apparently results from the liberal arts process, particularly in women's colleges. This might involve going on to graduate school.

He strongly recommends that we bring to bear the methods and the tools of social science on our planning and development of the whole educational process, for this offers a new resource and a more effective way of getting at some of the problems of the university student. And I would judge that he feels that the whole technique of testing ought to be more effectively and extensively used than it is at the present time, not for the purpose of attempting to change the course of the student or to put him on the spot in any way, but rather to give him the information, and background and understanding, that will make educational planning more effective and wiser.

He further indicated that we should, through these means and others, seek to account to a greater degree than we have for the changes that do occur in the course of college education. I judge that he has some feeling that we need not, indeed that we should not, take the gross picture, as, for example, might be reflected in the conclusions of the data that you had, Dr. Jacob, but rather we should look more at the difference between the first year and the fourth year and to break this down in order to get a better understanding of what is actually happening.

Finally, he made a strong plea for the development of a research department in our colleges in order to do the kinds of things that were proposed in these other conclusions. He felt that this kind of research department, operating in the humane atmosphere of the college environment, could be more effective than if it were operated externally to the college.

Is this a fair statement of your recommendations?

MR. SANFORD: Yes, very good.

CHAIRMAN KILLIAN: To me the central feature and the central concept of our discussion is that we are moving into a period when a preoccupation greater than we have been able to muster so far with individual differences, with the quality of the student, his motivation, his progress, his personality problems, is going to be of prime importance. This may be a lot more important than talking about enrollments. I should like to see us begin to move in this direction.

AMERICAN COUNCIL ON EDUCATION

ARTHUR S. ADAMS, *President*

The American Council on Education is a *council* of national educational associations; organizations having related interests; approved universities, colleges, teachers colleges, junior colleges, technological schools, and selected private secondary schools; state departments of education; city school systems and private school systems; selected educational departments of business and industrial companies; voluntary associations of higher education in the states; and large public libraries. It is a center of cooperation and coordination whose influence has been apparent in the shaping of American educational policies and the formation of educational practices during the past forty-one years.